THE
CALIF...
WINE COUNTRY
COOKBOOK II

COMPILED AND EDITED
by
Robert & Virginia Hoffman

The Cover: "Summer Vineyard"
by Ellie Marshall, Santa Rosa, Ca.

Typeset and proofread
by Nancy LaMothe, Sebastopol, Ca.

Printed by Griffin Printing Co.
Sacramento, Ca.

© 1993, 1994, 1995. The California Wine Country Cookbook II. All rights reserved. This book, or any portion thereof, may not be reproduced in any form, except for review purposes, without the written permission of The Hoffman Press, P.O. Box 2996, Santa Rosa, CA, 95405-0996.

Printed in the United States of America

ISBN # 0-9629927-6-3

"The California Wine Country"

Since the first printing of "The California Wine Country Cookbook," we have been asked repeatedly "Where and what is this California Wine Country?", "Why is the cuisine so unique?", "Who is responsible for all these wonderful foods?".

The California Wine Country is a country without geographic borders, whose citizens, a multi-ethnic group, are engaged in the growing, pressing and processing of grapes into wine. Because food is so closely paired with wine, it has always been of great importance here.

While the "native" population of growers and vintners has always been truly talented in the creation and preparation of food, "immigrants" from the entire world have come here in recent years, bringing their ethnic cuisines with them, both in ingredients and preparation.

The native and immigrant ingredients and recipes have merged to result in our "California Wine Country" becoming the center of creative cuisine whose chefs, both amateur and professional, have received international recognition for their skills in the use of common and uncommon ingredients in traditional and contemporary dishes.

The recipes of these chefs in our books are examples of the cuisine of "The California Wine Country".

We, the editors, dedicate this book to them: The Chefs of "The California Wine Country".

Robert and Virginia Hoffman, Santa Rosa, California, 1993.

Table of Contents

The California Wine Country, And How It Was Born

The California Wine Country was born in the late 1700s when Father Junipero Serra, a Catholic missionary priest, and his men built and settled a band of missions which ranged from San Diego north to Sonoma, sixty miles north of San Francisco. Requiring wine for the church masses, the missions had brought grapevine stock from Mexico (which came to be known as the Mission Variety Grape) and began making sacramental wine.

As the communities around the missions grew, there developed a market for wine and brandy by the settlers. Soon, as word spread to Europe of the wonderful soil and climate of California, ideal for the growing of wine grapes, vintners emigrated from France, Italy, Switzerland, Germany and Spain, bringing with them grapevine stock with which they were familiar.

The Buena Vista Winery, built in 1857 in the town of Sonoma, site of the northernmost mission in California, is considered to be the oldest premium winery in California. The cellars, dug into a limestone hill, are still in use and are open to visitors daily.

Most of these varieties took to their new home very well, developing slightly different flavors and bouquets, reflecting the soil and climactic conditions. These then became, "California Burgundy," "California Gamay," etc.

It was not until the completion of the transcontinental railroad in the late 1800s that the market for the wines of the state was expanded eastward to the Atlantic seaboard. They did not receive an enthusiastic reception. The East was accustomed to the wines of Europe and these "western wines" made very slow progress in penetrating the eastern market. It was not until California wines won gold medals at prestigious wine tastings in Europe, that these wines won the acceptance of the eastern seaboard. Soon, the wines of California became as acceptable to the American public as American-brewed beer.

The ratification of the Volstead Act by Congress in October of 1919, resulting in the enforcement of Prohibition throughout the United States, was devastating to the burgeoning wine industry of California. The great majority of the vineyards and wineries closed down overnight. A few, believing that the Volstead Act would be repealed, struggled along, making sacramental wine ... but many vineyards were plowed up and planted to other crops, or simply abandoned and left to grow wild.

Wineries sold their equipment for scrap metal in many cases, and fine oak barrels handcrafted in France for aging were cut up and sold for firewood.

When the law was repealed in 1934, a few wineries that did remain, rejoiced in the return of their market, but it was not to be for some time. The American public ... an entire generation ... had lost its taste or never acquired a taste for wine. For a considerable period after Repeal, the only wines that commanded any market in the United States were sweet dessert wines and brandy. Since then, America has learned to relish wine in its many roles: as the perfect accompaniment to food, as an aperitif, as a refreshing drink with minimal calories, and as an important ingredient in the preparation of food.

Today, in the 1990s, more than thirty different varieties of wine grapes cover more than 300,000 acres of California hills and valleys, with 700 wineries, ranging from the family owned and operated wineries that produce a few hundred cases, to the giants of the industry that produce millions of cases each year.

The 1990s brought, too, another attack by the phylloxera root louse, a vineyard parasite that attacks the roots of the grapevine and eventually kills it. In the late 19th century, this insect laid waste to thousands of acres of some of the finest vineyards in Europe and the United States. This time, a mutant strain of the insect is attacking what was believed to be immune rootstock here in California. It is conservatively estimated that it will cost a billion dollars or more to replant vineyards.

Fortunately, the replanting program is already underway and we are assured of a continuing supply of fine wines from California's vineyards.

Whether your preference is a jug table wine or a fine, aged wine, you will find it here in the California Wine Country. We hope that these recipes, gathered from those of us who live here, give you the same pleasure in making these dishes as it did for us in bringing them to you.

Contributors

*OUR APPRECIATION TO THE CHEFS,
WINEMAKERS, AND THE WINERIES FOR
SHARING SOME OF THEIR RECIPES WITH US.*

ADLER FELS WINERY
Ayn Ryan Coleman, Owner

ALEXANDER VALLEY VINEYARDS
Katie Wetzel Murphy

ALL SEASON'S CAFE
Mark Dierkhising, Chef & Owner

BARGETTO WINERY
Patricia Ballard, Senior Wine Counselor

BEAUCANON WINERY
Deborah Thorman, Hospitality Director

BERGFELD WINERY
Shanna Geiger

BELVEDERE WINERY
Gail Paquette, Chef

BERINGER VINEYARDS
Jerry Comfort, Executive Chef
Kerry Romaniello, Sous Chef

DUANE BUE

BUENA VISTA-CARNEROS ESTATE
Jill Davis, Winemaker

CARNEROS ALAMBIC DISTILLERY
Michele Mutrux

CHARLES SPINETTA WINERY
Laura Spinetta

CHATEAU ST. JEAN
Linda Hagen, Executive Chef

CHATEAU SOUVERAIN
Martin W. Courtman, Executive Chef

CHRISTOPHER CREEK WINERY
Susan Mitchell, President & Co-Owner

CLINE CELLARS
Deanna Williams, Chef
Niki Buchler, Cuisine Consultant

CLOS DU VAL WINERY
Mrs. Bernard Portet

CONCANNON VINEYARDS

CONN CREEK WINERY

CUVAISON WINERY

DE LOACH VINEYARDS
Christine De Loach
Michael Shafer, Executive Chef, Chez Melange

DOMAINE CHANDON
Philippe Jeanty, Chef de Cuisine

DRY CREEK VINEYARD
Brad Wallace

FERRARI-CARANO VINEYARDS & WINERY
Rhonda Carano, Co-Owner

FETZER VINEYARDS
John Ash, Culinary Director

FICKLIN VINEYARDS
Shirley Sarvis, Consultant

FOPPIANO VINEYARDS
Susan Foppiano

FRANCISCAN VINEYARDS

FREEMARK ABBEY VINEYARD
Sandra Learned, Consulting Chef

J. FRITZ WINERY

GLEN ELLEN WINERY
Stella Fleming, Executive Chef

GLORIA FERRER CHAMPAGNE CAVES

GREENWOOD RIDGE VINEYARDS
Dony Kwan

GRGICH HILLS CELLAR
Violet Grgich

GREYSTONE CELLARS

GUENOC WINERY
Karen Melander-Magoon

HEITZ WINE CELLARS
Kathleen Heitz

HOP KILN WINERY AT GRIFFIN VINEYARD

INGLENOOK-NAPA VALLEY
Jamie Morningstar

KENDALL-JACKSON VINEYARDS

KENWOOD VINEYARDS

KONOCTI WINERY
Madelene Lyon, Consulting Chef

KORBEL CHAMPAGNE CELLARS
Teresa Douglas/Mitchell, Culinary Director

KOZLOWSKI FARMS
Carmen Kozlowski
Carol Kozlowski-Every

KUNDE ESTATE WINERY
Pat Roney, President, Leslie Kunde
Marcia Kunde Mickelson, David Noyes, Winemaker

LAKE SONOMA WINERY
Kate Moore

LANDMARK VINEYARDS

J. LOHR WINERY
Christopher Majer,Chef, Splendido Restaurant
Chef Victor Rallo

LOUIS M. MARTINI WINERY

MCDOWELL VALLEY VINEYARDS
Richard Keehn, Proprietor
Karen Keehn, Proprietor

MARK WEST WINERY
Carolann Heyden
Eunice Marion

MARTINELLI VINEYARDS
Julie Martinelli

MARTINI & PRATI WINES
Jeani Martini

MATANZAS CREEK WINERY
Sarah Kaswan, Chef

MERRYVALE VINEYARDS
Robert Levy, Winemaker

MIRASSOU

MONTICELLO CELLARS
David Lawson, Chef

MUMM CUVÉE NAPA
Elaine Bell

MURPHY-GOODE ESTATE WINERY
Mary Lannin

NAVARRO VINEYARDS

J. PEDRONCELLI WINERY
Christine Pedroncelli

PEJU PROVINCE WINERY
Herta Peju, Owner

PERRY CREEK VINEYARDS
Alice Chazen, Owner

PIPER SONOMA
Michael Hirschberg & Sheila Parrott, Ristorante Siena

QUIVERA VINEYARDS
Holly P. Wendt, Proprietor

RAVENSWOOD WINERY
Joel Peterson, Winemaker

RAYMOND VINEYARDS & CELLAR
Virginia Raymond
Walter Raymond

ROBERT MONDAVI WINERY
Annie Roberts, Chef

RODNEY STRONG VINEYARDS
Lucy Cafaro
Bea Beasley

ROEDERER ESTATE

ROUDIN SMITH VINEYARDS
Annamaria Roudin

RUSSIAN RIVER VINEYARDS RESTAURANT
Robert Engel, Chef
Christine Topolos

ST. FRANCIS VINEYARDS & WINERY
Penny Cassina
Terrye Temple

ST. SUPÉRY VINEYARDS & WINERY
Jamie Purviance

V. SATTUI WINERY
Robert O'Malley, Operations Manager

SAUSAL WINERY
Cindy Martin & Roselee Demonstene, Co-Owners

SCHARFFENBERGER CELLARS
Kazuto Matsusaka, Chinois on Main Restaurant

SCHUG CARNEROS ESTATE WINERY
Kristine Schug

SEBASTIANI VINEYARDS
Sylvia Sebastiani

SIMI WINERY
Mary Evely, Chef

SMOTHERS BROS. WINES
The Tasting Room Staff

SONOMA CHEESE FACTORY

STERLING VINEYARDS
Richard Alexei, Food & Wine Consultant

SUTTER HOME WINERY
National Burger Cook-off Winners

TORRES VINEYARD & WINERY
Marimar Torres, President

WEIBEL VINEYARDS
Diana Weibel

WENTE BROS WINE CELLARS & RESTAURANT
Kimball Jones, Executive Chef

WINDSOR VINEYARDS

Cooking With Wine
Some Guidelines That May Help You

The most important guide in choosing which wine to use as an ingredient in which dish ... is you. Try some of the guidelines that we have noted here ... and then, based upon that, broaden your range by trying different wines in different proportions in different dishes. But, remember a few things. First, taste the wine you are going to use in cooking. If it tastes good, use it. If you don't like the taste, don't use it. Cooking will not hide the taste that you don't like; it will intensify it.

Second, the price of the wine does not make it, necessarily, a great wine for cooking. Great subtleties in bouquets and multiple flavors are often diminished when subjected to heat with herbs, spices, etc.

Finally, serve the same wine that you used as an ingredient, if at all possible. If the wine you are serving is a rare vintage wine, use a wine of the same varietal as an ingredient (a good wine, yes, but not necessarily a fine, old vintage wine). Remember, too, that wine as an ingredient in cooking is meant to enhance the dish ... not dominate it.

	WINE	QUANTITY
SOUPS		
Cream, Clear	Dry Sherry	1 teaspoon per portion
Vegetable, Meat	Red, White	1 teaspoon per portion
MEATS		
Beef	Red, Brandy	1/4 cup per pound
Lamb, Veal	White	1/4 cup per pound
Ham, Baked	White, Port	2 cups (baste)
Kidneys, etc.	White	1/4 cup per pound
PASTAS		
Tomato Sauce	Red	1/4 cup per portion
Cream Sauce	White	1/4 cup per portion

	WINE	QUANTITY
POULTRY		
Chicken, Roasted	White	1/2 cup per pound (baste)
Chicken, Poached	White	1/2 cup per pound
Turkey, Roasted	White, Red	1/2 cup per pound (baste)
Cornish Game Hen	White, Red	1/4 cup per pound (baste)
Duck	Red, Brandy	1/4 cup per pound (baste)
SEAFOOD		
Fish, Broiled	Dry White	1/4 cup per pound
Fish, Poached	Dry White	1/4 cup per pound
Fish, Baked	Dry White	1/4 cup per pound
Fish, Sauteed	Dry White	4 tablespoons per pound
Shellfish	Dry White	1/4 cup per pound
FRUITS & VEGETABLES		
Fresh Fruit	Champagne, White	To taste
Cooked Vegetables	Dry White	To taste
Salads	White, Red	To taste

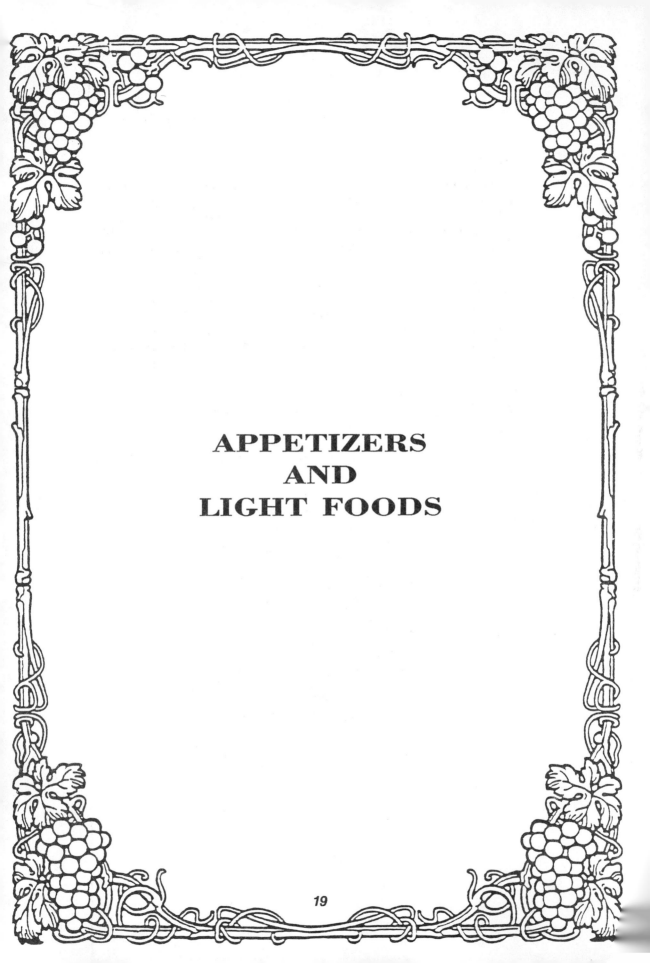

APPETIZERS
AND
LIGHT FOODS

Sonoma Goat Cheese and Sundried Tomato Strudel

1 box Phyllo dough
1/2 cup olive oil
8 ounces goat or Feta cheese
1/2 cup sundried tomatoes, 1/2-inch diced (soak in hot water if salty)
1/4 cup diced, pitted Kalmata Greek Olives

2 tablespoons chopped basil
1 teaspoon black pepper
2 tablespoons toasted pine nuts
Fresh baby salad greens, tossed with Balsamic vinegar and olive oil

Thaw the phyllo dough; lay out 1 sheet and brush with olive oil. Overlap another sheet on top and brush with olive oil again. Repeat one more time.

Dice the cheese into 3/4-inch dices and toss with the diced sundried tomatoes, basil, olives, black pepper and pine nuts. Spoon a row of this mixture on the bottom edge of the phyllo. Roll the phyllo up and cut into desired portion size. Brush exterior with olive oil and place on a cookie sheet in the center of a preheated 425 degree oven until golden brown, approximately 8 to 10 minutes.

Place on a salad plate and surround with baby greens. Serves 4.

Wine Suggestion: Serve as a first course with Beringer Sauvignon Blanc or as a main course with Beringer Private Reserve Cabernet Sauvignon or Knights Valley Cabernet Sauvignon.

Jerry Comfort, Executive Chef
Beringer Vineyards

A native Californian, Jerry Comfort has been with some of the most highly respected restaurants in California. He began as the chef at Eppaminondas Restaurant, then sous chef at Fourneau's Ovens at the Stanford Court, leaving there to help open Masa's Restaurant, then to work with Jeremiah Tower at Stars and the Santa Fe Bar & Grill.

His next project was as chef de cuisine at Domaine Chandon, followed by serving as executive chef at the award winning Checkers in Los Angeles. The lure of the Napa Valley was overpowering, and in 1991 he became executive chef of Beringer Vineyards.

Wild Rice Pancakes with Candied Onions

WILD RICE PANCAKES:

1 cup milk
1/4 teaspoon salt
1 tablespoon melted butter
1 teaspoon fresh thyme, chopped
1 each small red and green bell
pepper, finely diced

1 cup cooked wild rice
2 eggs, separated
1 cup flour
Salt and pepper to taste

Mix together milk, rice, salt and pepper, thyme and peppers. Beat egg yolks and add to rice mixture, stir in flour and butter. Beat egg whites until stiff, gently fold whites into rice mixture. Tablespoon mixture on to a flat griddle or a non-stick pan at medium to medium-high heat. Top with candied onions. Approximately 30 pancakes.

CANDIED ONIONS:

2 white onions, peeled and sliced
 paper thin
1 cup sugar

1 cup raspberry vinegar
1 cup balsamic vinegar

Combine vinegar and sugar in saute pan and bring to a boil. Add onion and cook until almost dry. Cool.

Enjoy with Monticello Cellars Estate Pinot Noir.

David Lawson, Chef
Monticello Cellars

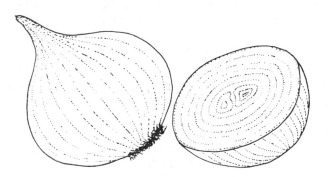

Grilled Thai Sweetwater Prawns Wrapped in Proscuitto

12 pieces paper-thin prosciutto
20 to 25 large raw prawns, peeled
and deveined
1/4 cup honey
2 tablespoons dry sherry

2 tablespoons fresh lime juice
Healthy pinch of each: curry
powder, tumeric, coriander,
dry ginger, paprika, cumin,
chili powder and cayenne

Cut prosciutto in half lengthwise and set aside. (If too thin, leave whole.) Put prawns, honey, sherry, lime juice and all the spices in a glass dish and marinate 2 to 3 hours in refrigerator, stirring occasionally. Wrap each prawn with a strip of prosciutto and place on a small skewer, 2 prawns per skewer. Brush again with marinade and put on a hot grill, 2 to 3 minutes each side. Serves 6 to 8.

Delicious with our Matanzas Creek Sauvignon Blanc.

Sarah Kaswan, Chef
Matanzas Creek Winery

Hot Crab Dip

4 6-ounce cans crabmeat
1/2 cup onion, minced
1 tablespoon jalapeno mustard
1/4 cup Chardonnay

1 cup mayonnaise
2 tablespoons lemon juice
8 ounces cream cheese,
softened

Beat cream cheese until smooth. Add crabmeat (2 cans drained, 2 cans with juice). Add 1/4 cup Chardonnay. Cook in greased ovenproof dish at 350 degrees for 30 minutes. Makes 3 cups. Serve with crackers or French bread. Good warm or cold. Serves 10.

Serve with Martinelli's Chardonnay.

Julie Martinelli
Martinelli Vineyards

Corn Griddle-Cakes with Avocado and Smoked Chicken

1/2 cup corn kernels (fresh or frozen)
1/2 cup cornmeal
1/2 cup boiling water
1/2 cup flour
1/2 teaspoon salt

2 teaspoons baking powder
1 egg
1/2 cup milk
2 ounces butter, melted
Butter for cooking

Puree the corn kernels in a food processor or chop well with a knife, then mash with a wooden spoon. Combine cornmeal and boiling water and stir until water is absorbed. Add pureed corn, flour, salt, baking powder, and milk, and whisk. Add egg and butter and whisk just until all ingredients are well combined. The batter may be made up to an hour in advance.

Heat a large skillet or griddle and brush with melted butter. Pour about 1 tablespoon of batter for each -- remember, they're finger food, so keep them small. When the top begins to solidify, flip the cake (a narrow, flexible blade spatula is best for this). Adjust heat so that both sides brown nicely. Transfer to a warm oven and continue until all batter is used. Yield: about 35 griddle cakes 1 1/2 inches in diameter.

SMOKED CHICKEN:

2 cups chopped smoked chicken
1 tablespoon mayonnaise
2 teaspoons Dijon mustard

Note: Smoked chickens are widely available in meat markets, delicatessens and specialty shops. If not obtainable, smoked turkey breast is the closest substitute.

Combine chicken, mustard and mayonnaise. Should your smoked chicken be dry, a little more mayonnaise may be necessary. This can be prepared in advance and refrigerated, but let it warm a little before using.

AVOCADO:

2 medium ripe Haas avocados
Lemon

Cut the avocados in half, remove the pit and scoop out the flesh with a spoon. In a bowl, mash the avocados and a few drops of lemon juice with a fork. It should be a little lumpy. Do not add salt since this component is meant to balance the saltiness of smoked chicken. Place a piece of plastic wrap directly on the avocado puree to keep it from darkening. It's best not to mash the avocados more than an hour or two in advance.

TO ASSEMBLE:

Spread each warm griddle-cake with a teaspoon of the avocado, then top with a tablespoon of the smoked chicken. A tiny parsley leaf can garnish each.

This tasty hors d'oeuvre offers an unusual and delightful combination of flavors and textures.

1988 Sterling Vineyards' Lake Chardonnay accompanies this dish.

Richard Alexei, Food & Wine Consultant
Sterling Vineyards

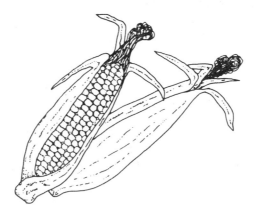

Grilled Polenta with Fontina Cheese, Shiitake Mushrooms and Sun-Dried Tomatoes

4 cups water
1 cup polenta or yellow corn meal
1 tablespoon minced fresh parsley
1/2 cup green onions, minced
1/2 cup mushrooms, minced
Salt and pepper
1/4 pound Fontina cheese, thinly sliced
1/2 cup dry white wine

1/4 pound (1 stick) butter
2 teaspoons ground white pepper
1 teaspoon fresh thyme or oregano (use 1/2 if using dry herbs)
Shiitake mushrooms and sun-dried tomatoes for garnish

Bring water, salt, pepper and thyme to a boil in large saucepan. Slowly beat in polenta with a whisk to avoid lumps. Reduce heat to low and stir to prevent sticking. Cook slowly for 10 minutes. In a separate pan, saute mushrooms and green onions in 2 tablespoons of butter until cooked through and just beginning to brown. Season with a little salt and pepper, add wine and reduce until most of the wine cooks away. Add to polenta mixture with remaining butter and parsley.

Off heat, spread polenta mixture on buttered cake pan or cookie sheet so that it is approximately 1/2 inch thick. Cool, cover with plastic and refrigerate up to a day in advance. To complete the dish, cut polenta into diamonds or other interesting shapes.

Grill over mesquite until surface is lightly toasted. Turn, place a slice of Fontina cheese on top and allow to just melt. Serve warm, garnished with grilled shiitake mushrooms and slivers of sun-dried tomatoes. Serves 6 to 8.

Serve with Martini Zinfandel.

Louis M. Martini Winery

Crostini with Goat Cheese, Sundried Tomatoes and a Basil Leaf

4 medium sundried tomato halves in oil
2 tablespoons oil from the tomatoes (or olive oil)

8 ounces young goat cheese
Fresh basil leaves
32 crostini (below)

Combine the sundried tomatoes, oil and goat cheese in a food processor and puree. The mixture will be a brilliant pink color. There should be no large pieces of tomato remaining. The mixture can be prepared in advance and refrigerated for several days. On each crostini, place a small basil leaf (or half of a large one) on one side. Smear a dollop of the goat cheese on the other side, coming half-way up the leaf. You can pipe the cheese on decoratively with a forcing bag if you want to be more formal. These hold very well and you can assemble them 1/2 hour in advance.

CROSTINI:

French bread baguette
4 tablespoons olive oil

Slice the baguette 1/8 to 1/4 inch thick. Brush the slices lightly with olive oil. Arrange on a baking sheet and toast in a 425 degree oven until nicely browned. When cool, they should be totally dry and crisp. Return any that are moist to a hot oven for another minute. These crostini can be made well in advance, even stored airtight for several days. If they get limp from humidity, a few seconds in a hot oven will re-crisp them.

I suggest Sterling Vineyards 1989 Sauvignon Blanc to accompany this dish.

Richard Alexei, Food & Wine Consultant
Sterling Vineyards

Bruschetta
(Toasted Tomato Bread)

6 slices Italian bread (cut 3/4 inch thick)
1 clove garlic
2 tablespoons extra virgin olive oil
1/2 pound ripe tomatoes, coarsely chopped*
1/2 cup red onion, finely chopped

8 fresh basil leaves, coarsely chopped
1 tablespoon oregano leaves, finely chopped
Salt and freshly ground black pepper

Lightly toast the bread. Rub one side of the toast with garlic clove. Drizzle olive oil over each slice.

Mix together tomatoes, onion and basil. Spread mixture over each slice. Sprinkle oregano, salt and pepper on top.

Bake in a 350 degree oven about 10 minutes. (Do not burn edges of toast.)

Serve immediately. Serves 6 as appetizer.

*Note: This appetizer is best made only when red vine-ripened tomatoes are in season.

Suggested wine: V. Sattui Suzanne's Vineyard Zinfandel or Monastero Le Vallesi Chianti Classico.

Robert O'Malley, Operations Manager
V. Sattui Winery

Susan's Sundried Tomato Tapanade

1 cup sundried tomatoes, re-hydrate in boiling water for 1 minute
5 cloves garlic, peeled
1/4 cup extra virgin olive oil
1 tablespoon balsamic vinegar

1 teaspoon dried thyme or 1 tablespoon fresh
1 teaspoon fresh rosemary
10-15 Kalamata Greek olives, pitted
Salt and pepper to taste

While tomatoes are still hot from re-hydrating, strain. In food processor, combine sundried tomatoes, garlic, olive oil, herbs, olives and vinegar. Blend until well mixed. More oil can be added for more spreadable consistency. Capers can be added after blending - they add a nice taste and color. Keep covered in refrigerator (unless you want everything to taste of garlic). Will keep for several weeks.

Serve as we do, on French bread, but it is also great with grilled chicken, added to pasta, soups and chili. The most important thing to remember is to always serve this with a full-bodied delicious red wine - a nice bottle of Christopher Creek Petite Sirah comes to mind!

Susan Mitchell
President and Co-Owner
Christopher Creek Winery

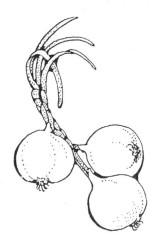

Mushrooms a la Gloria

6 tablespoons butter, room temperature
1 tablespoon minced garlic
1 1/2 pounds mushrooms, cleaned and stemmed

1 1/2 cups Brut sparkling wine
Salt and pepper to taste
1 to 2 tablespoons minced fresh parsley or mixed fresh herbs

In 10-inch skillet, melt 3 tablespoons of the butter over medium heat; add garlic. Cook and stir garlic until lightly browned, add mushrooms. Cook, stirring occasionally, until lightly browned, about 5 minutes. Add Brut, bring to a boil. Reduce heat, simmer until liquid is reduced to 1/3 cup, about 10 minutes. Taste and adjust seasoning with salt and pepper. Remove from heat; whisk in remaining butter until sauce is slightly thickened.

Arrange mushrooms in serving dish with toothpicks inserted in each. Pour sauce over and garnish with minced parsley or fresh herbs. Serves 6. Gloria Ferrer Brut (NV) is suggested.

Gloria Ferrer Champagne Caves

Summer Salsa

1 cup kiwi, chopped small
1 cup red onion, chopped small
2 cups tomatillos, chopped small
2 cups ripe tomatoes, chopped small
2 cups ripe melon, any combination of cantaloupe, honeydew, crenshaw

Juice of 2 lemons
Juice of 2 limes
4 tablespoons peanut oil
2 bunches cilantro, chopped
1/2 cup chopped Jalapeno chilies
Salt and pepper to taste

Combine and serve with chips or over grilled foods.

We suggest Smothers 1989 Chardonnay as a wonderful wine with this appetizer.

Smothers Tasting Room Staff
Smothers Bros. Wines

Sonoma Goat Cheese Torta

1 pound mild goat cheese (cream
cheese may be substituted)
1/2 pound unsalted butter
6 ounces sundried tomatoes
 packed in oil, drained
2 cups basil, firmly packed

4 cloves of garlic
1/2 teaspoon salt
1/2 teaspoon pepper
1/3 cup olive oil
Plastic wrap

In a food processor, combine goat cheese and butter until well blended, set aside. In food processor, chop sundried tomatoes, set aside. In food processor, place basil, garlic, salt and pepper. With motor running, slowly drizzle in the oil through the feed tube, and process until the basil is pureed, set aside.

Line 3 cup mold or loaf pan with plastic wrap. Spread 1/3 of the goat cheese mixture in bottom of the mold. Spread with 1/2 cup of the basil mixture. Top with another 1/3 of the goat cheese mixture. Spread with sundried tomatoes. Top with remaining goat cheese. Refrigerate until firm, at least 1 hour.

To serve, unmold onto serving plate and spread on crackers or toasted garlic croutons (slices of baguettes, oven toasted with garlic butter). Serves 8.

You'll enjoy Benziger of Glen Ellen Cabernet Sauvignon with this.

Stella Fleming, Executive Chef
Glen Ellen Winery

Goat Cheese Cake

FILLING:

12 ounces goat cheese
16 ounces cream cheese
3 eggs
1/2 teaspoon chopped fresh
 rosemary
1/2 teaspoon chopped fresh
 marjoram

1/2 teaspoon chopped fresh
 thyme
1 teaspoon chopped fresh
 parsley
1/2 cup pine nuts

CRUST:

1 1/2 cups flour
1 stick butter
Pinch of salt
3 tablespoons cold water

Place crust in tarte pan and line with parchment. Fill with pie weights and bake in a 350 degree oven for 30 minutes.

Blend room temperature cheese, add eggs one at a time, add herbs. Fill crust with cheese filling, sprinkle with pine nuts and bake in a 350 degree oven for 30 to 45 minutes until firm. Cool to room temperature.

Recommended wine: Chateau St. Jean Fumé Blanc.

Linda Hagen, Executive Chef
Chateau St. Jean

Leek and Cheese Tart

DOUGH:

1 cup all purpose flour
4 ounces butter, frozen and cut
  into 1/2-inch pieces

4 tablespoons ice water
Pinch salt
1 egg yolk

In a food processor, pulse flour and butter until mixture resembles coarse corn meal. In a small bowl, mix together water, salt and egg yolk, then add to food processor. Whirl until dough comes together into a ball. Wrap ball in plastic. Refrigerate two hours or overnight.

FILLING:

1 tablespoon olive oil
2 cloves garlic, minced
2 pounds of leeks, thinly sliced
1/2 teaspoon fresh ground black
 pepper
1 tablespoon fresh thyme, finely
chopped

3/4 teaspoon salt
1/2 cup milk
3 egg yolks
3 ounces mild goat cheese,
  crumbled into small pieces
2 ounces asiago cheese,
grated

In a large pot, heat oil over medium high heat. Add garlic and cook gently until aroma is apparent (about 1 minute). Bring heat to low. Add leeks and cook, stirring every few minutes, until all liquid has evaporated (about 45 minutes to an hour). Don't allow browning. Transfer garlic and leeks to a large bowl. Add pepper, salt and thyme. Let mixture cool. In a small bowl, blend thoroughly milk, egg yolks, goat cheese and asiago cheese. Add to the leek mixture. Blend well. Refrigerate until ready to use.

Preheat oven to 425 degrees. Roll out dough thinly and line a 9-inch tart pan (1-inch sides) with removable bottom. Remove excess dough. Prick with fork several times. Line shell with parchment paper and fill with dried beans. Bake in a 425 degree oven for 10 minutes. Remove paper and beans. Bake for 5 more minutes, until lightly golden brown. Remove from oven. Lower temperature to 375 degrees.

Pour filling into shell. Bake in a 375 degree oven for 45 minutes, or until cheese browns on top. Serve warm or at room temperature.

Serve with St. Supéry Merlot.

Jamie Purviance
St. Supéry Vineyards & Winery

Prawns in Pancetta

36 prawns   36 slices pancetta (thin)

Peel and clean prawns. Wrap prawns in pancetta. Grill or pan fry until cooked through, about 3 minutes per side. Serve with Sundried Tomato Vinaigrette (see recipe below). Serves 6.

SUNDRIED TOMATO VINAIGRETTE:

1 cup olive oil   1 cup finely chopped oil-cured
1/4 cup balsamic vinegar   sundried tomatoes
                                             2 cloves garlic, minced

Heat sundried tomatoes and minced garlic in olive oil until warm. Remove from heat. Add balsamic vinegar and, using a wire whisk, blend thoroughly.

Serve with Piper Sonoma 1982 Brut Reserve.

Michael Hirschberg and Shiela Parrott, Ristorante Siena
for
Piper Sonoma

SOUPS

Tomato and Cilantro Soup

Preparation time is 60 minutes

1/8 cup olive oil
2 medium yellow onions, rough
 chop
3 1/2 pounds canned plum
 tomatoes, crushed or whole
8 large cloves garlic, peeled

1 quart chicken stock
1 bay leaf
1 cup fresh cilantro, rough
 chop
Salt and pepper to taste
Sour cream and tortilla chips,
 optional

Heat the olive oil in a large soup pan that can contain all ingredients. Saute the onions until soft. Add the tomatoes, garlic, chicken stock and bay leaf and simmer for 1 hour.

Add the cilantro and cook for 2 minutes. Puree in a food processor and strain through a sieve. Season with salt and pepper.

At this point, you can freeze the soup in small serving-size containers and thaw out as desired. For every 2 cups of puree that you reheat, add 1/2 cup of milk when the puree is simmering. Serve immediately.

You can also garnish the soup with a dollop of sour cream and crushed tortilla chips if you desire.

Serve with Inglenook-Napa Valley, Estate Bottled Gravion.

Jamie Morningstar
Inglenook-Napa Valley

Jamie Morningstar, former Resident Chef at Inglewood-Napa, comes by her interest in food and wine from both her grandfather, John Daniel, Jr., and his uncle, her great grand uncle, Gustave Niebaum, who founded the winery in 1879. A graduate of the California Culinary Academy, she was executive sous chef at the Meadowood Resort in the Napa Valley before joining Inglenook Napa. She has left to pursue her career studies in Europe.

Cream of Sorrel Soup

1 tablespoon olive oil, preferably extra virgin
2 cloves garlic, crushed and peeled
1/4 pound fresh sorrel, coarsely chopped

1 1/2 teaspoon salt
Freshly ground black pepper
1 quart chicken stock
1 egg
1/4 cup heavy cream

In a medium saucepan, heat the olive oil, add the garlic, and let it color lightly. Add the sorrel and salt and pepper and stir to wilt the sorrel, about one minute. Add the stock and simmer for about 15 minutes.

Puree the soup in a food processor or blender, half at a time, for about two minutes. Return it to the saucepan and keep it warm -- not quite at a simmer.

Just before serving, whisk the egg in a bowl until it doubles in volume. Slowly whisk in the cream. When the two are thoroughly incorporated, gradually add the mixture to the hot -- but not close to boiling -- soup. Continue whisking until the soup is slightly thickened, but still light.

Serve immediately in individual heated soup tureens. Serves 4.

The tartness of fresh sorrel in this autumn soup complements the youthful acidity of our 1990 Chardonnay. Try it as a satisfying first course to a holiday meal.

Robert O'Malley, Operations Manager
V. Sattui Winery

Potato and Leek Soup

2 medium onions
2 pounds potatoes
1 pound leeks
2 tablespoons unsalted butter
1 bay leaf
3 cups milk
Salt and pepper to taste

Garnish:
1/2 cup heavy cream
  (optional)
2 tablespoons chopped fresh
  chives

Slice the onions. Wash and slice the potatoes and leeks. Melt the butter in a large saucepan over a low heat. Add the onions, potatoes, leeks, and bay leaf to the saucepan. Cover and simmer 10 minutes. Add the milk and seasonings and simmer for 30 more minutes, until the vegetables are tender. Remove the bay leaf and serve, garnished with the cream and chives.

Note: Alternately, the soup may be pureed in a blender, taking care not to puree it beyond the desired texture, and served with a garnish of cream and chives. Delicious either hot or chilled. Serves 4 to 6.

Serve with Concannon Vineyard Chardonnay.

Concannon Vineyards

Corn and Red Pepper Soup

2 red bell peppers
3 tablespoons butter
1 onion, chopped
4 cups corn

4 cups chicken stock
1 cup heavy cream
Salt and pepper
Pinch of cayenne

Saute onion in butter 5 minutes; do not brown. Add corn and saute 5 minutes. Add stock and simmer 15 minutes. Puree. Add cream, salt and pepper and cayenne to taste. Skin and puree red peppers. Serve soup with a dollop of red pepper puree.

Linda Hagen, Executive Chef
Chateau St. Jean

Harvest Soup

4 tablespoons butter
1/2 medium onion, minced
2 shallots, minced
1 stalk celery
1 carrot, peeled and minced
1 teaspoon fresh chives
2 cups canned pumpkin
2 teaspoons grated orange zest

2 dashes hot red pepper
 sauce
2 cups chicken broth
1 cup half & half
1/2 cup heavy cream
1/4 cup orange juice
1/4 cup Chardonnay
1 cup sour cream
3/4 teaspoon salt

Heat butter in medium saucepan over medium heat. Add onions, shallots, celery and carrot. Cook, stirring constantly until softened, about 7 minutes. Stir in pumpkin and chicken broth; simmer uncovered 10 minutes.

Transfer to blender or food processor and puree until smooth. Return to sauce pan. Stir in half & half, cream, orange juice and Chardonnay. Heat until lightly boiling. Reduce heat and simmer uncovered for 10 minutes. Meanwhile, combine sour cream, chives and orange zest in a small bowl. Season soup with salt and red pepper sauce and top each serving with a dollop of sour cream mixture. Serves 6.

Jill Davis, Winemaker
Buena Vista-Carneros Estate

Curried Chicken and Olive Soup

1 2 1/2-3 pound broiling chicken
2 large onions, sliced thin
2 large tart apples, sliced
1 can of peas, including liquid
2/3 cup of green stuffed olives, chopped
3 cups of milk
2 stalks of celery, cut in pieces

1/2 teaspoon salt
1 teaspoon chili powder
1 teaspoon curry powder
1/2 cup all purpose flour
1/4 pound margarine or butter
1 cup cream
1 medium onion, cut in pieces

Boil chicken in 4 cups of water, with the medium onion pieces and the 2 stalks of celery for approximately one hour until tender. Cool and drain. Strain broth and put aside 3 cups. Dice chicken to total approximately 1 1/2 to 2 cups. Fry the remaining onions and apples in margarine or butter, adding the salt, chili powder, curry powder and flour. Stir well. Now add the chicken broth and the peas. Cook until tender, stirring frequently. Now add the milk, diced chicken and chopped olives. Bring to a boil and add cream. Serve hot, immediately. Serves 6 to 8 persons.

A dry white wine is appropriate for this, when served as a main course.

Admittedly a very unusual combination of ingredients, but well worth the effort, resulting in a very, very good soup...easily a main course when served with a mixed green salad and crusty French bread. VMH

Cream of Golden Zucchini Soup
with Roasted Garlic

2 large onions, cut into 1/2-inch dice
8 6-inch golden zucchinis, sliced into 1/2-inch rounds
1/4 cup mashed roasted garlic cloves (approx 1 head)
1 stick unsalted butter
3 cups chicken or vegetable stock
1 cup heavy cream

Salt and freshly ground white pepper to taste
Garnishes: sour cream, fresh tomato concasse, (peeled, seeded and chopped tomato pulp)
Fresh basil, in chiffonnade form (thin shreds)

In a heavy bottomed 4-quart pot, saute the onions in the butter over medium heat until they begin to brown. Add zucchini slices, roasted garlic and stock, and allow mixture to simmer until zucchini slices are completely soft, about 25 minutes.

Allow mixture to cool slightly (10 to 15 minutes) and then puree in a blender or processor. Put pureed soup back into pot, stir in cream, and add desired amount of salt and freshly ground white pepper. Heat soup just to the boiling point and serve while hot.

Ladle soup into serving bowls and place a dollop of sour cream into center of each bowl. Sprinkle a few tomatoes and some of the basil over the center of each bowl. Serve immediately. Serves 4 to 6.

Serve with Schug 1990 Carneros Chardonnay.

Kristine Schug
Schug Carneros Estate Winery

Hearty Spring Vegetable Chowder with Ham

3 strips of chopped bacon
6 cups chicken stock
2 medium sliced brown onions
6 garlic cloves, minced
3 stalks 1/4-inch sliced celery
3 10-inch carrots sliced 1/4 inch
2 large peeled and cubed brown
 potatoes
2 teaspoons cumin
1 teaspoon salt
Dash Cayenne

1 1/4 pounds cured ham
1 pound broccoli flowerettes
1/2 pound green beans,
 trimmed into thirds
2 medium tomatoes, seeded,
 cut into chunks
8 ounces halved mushrooms
8 1/2 ounces corn (canned or
 fresh), drained
2 tablespoons olive oil

In a large stock pot, cook bacon until brown. Remove bacon pieces, set aside. Add olive oil. Saute onions, garlic and celery until tender, stir approximately 5 minutes. Add potatoes, stir 10 minutes. Add chicken stock. Transfer 1/2 of mixture to food processor, puree until smooth. Return to stock pot. Add remaining vegetables and season with spices. Bring to a slow boil. Reduce to simmer, uncovered for approximately 40 minutes or until vegetables are tender. Add ham and bacon bits. Season to taste. Serves 6 to 8.

Jill Davis, Winemaker
Buena Vista-Carneros Estate

Cream of Avocado Soup

4 large ripe avocados
3 cups chicken broth
1/2 teaspoon salt

Pinch white pepper
1/2 teaspoon Worcestershire
1 cup light cream

Peel, pit and cube avocados, then puree in blender. In a saucepan, mix avocado puree, chicken broth, salt, pepper and Worcestershire. Heat to boiling point, stirring occasionally. Stir in 1 cup light cream. Cover and simmer 10 minutes. Serve soup hot; garnish each bowl with croutons or popcorn. Serves 6.

This is one from my own file and I use it frequently when avocados are in season. Try to get the large Haas type, if possible. VMH

Butternut-Shrimp Bisque

1 butternut squash (you need
   about 4 cups of cooked puree)
   from the butternut squash
1/2 cup unsalted butter
1 cup diced onion
1/2 cup flour

6 cups chicken stock
1 cup dry Chenin Blanc
1 cup whipping cream
1/4 cup chopped fresh parsley
1 pound small uncooked
   shrimp

Peel the butternut squash and remove the seeds. Dice the squash into 1-inch squares. Steam squash until tender. Puree cooked squash and measure 4 cups of puree - set aside.

Melt butter in a heavy saucepan over medium heat. Add onion and cook until transparent - stir occasionally. Add flour and cook about 3 minutes. Gradually add stock while stirring. Bring to a boil. Add pureed butternut squash. Add wine, stir, then add cream. Heat until almost boiling. Add shrimp and stir just until shrimp turn pink. Quickly stir in parsley and serve. Serves 6.

Enjoy with a glass of Charles Spinetta Dry Chenin Blanc!

Laura Spinetta
Charles Spinetta Winery

J. Fritz Winery Minestrone

INGREDIENTS:

4 strips bacon, diced
1 tablespoon olive oil
1 tablespoon balsamic vinegar
2 tablespoons tomato paste
3 cups Zinfandel
12 cups beef stock (may use
 quality canned beef broth)
1 8-ounce can garbanzo beans,
 use liquid

1 8-ounce can kidney beans,
 use liquid
1 tablespoon salt
1 teaspoon pepper
1 tablespoon oregano
4 bay leaves
2/3 cup small elbow macaroni

THE VEGETABLES:

6 large cloves garlic, minced
3 large onions, chopped
2 leeks, white part only, chopped
1 cup celery including leaves,
 chopped
2 pounds plum tomatoes, peeled
 and chopped

4 carrots, slices
2 zucchini, quartered lengthwise and sliced
1/2 small cabbage, shredded
1 bunch spinach, leaves only,
 coarsely chopped
Freshly grated imported
 Parmesan cheese for garnish

In a large skillet, fry bacon in olive oil until cooked, but not crisp. Remove bacon from pan and reserve. Saute the onion, celery, leeks and garlic in skillet until limp. Add the tomato paste and vinegar, stirring until well blended with the vegetables, and mixture begins to bubble. Add one cup of Zinfandel and stir until well blended. Bring to boil and remove from heat.

In large pot, place remaining tomatoes, beans, parsley, carrots, the saute mixture, salt, pepper, oregano and bay leaves. Mix well and bring to a boil. Lower heat and simmer for 1 hour. Add zucchini, cabbage and pasta. Simmer an additional 30 minutes. Add spinach and simmer for 20 minutes. Serve topped with Parmesan cheese.

Serve with our Zinfandel.

J. Fritz Winery

Winter Vegetable Soup

1/4 cup olive oil
3 large leeks, white part only,
thinly sliced
1 clove garlic, chopped
4 large baking potatoes
4 carrots

1 yellow squash
4 cups chicken stock
  (homemade or canned)
Nutmeg
Salt and pepper

Pour the olive oil in a large soup pot and saute the sliced leeks and garlic in the oil over medium heat. Meanwhile, peel and dice the remaining vegetables. when the leeks and garlic are soft and golden, pour the chicken stock into the soup pot with them. Then add the diced vegetables and cook over high heat, careful not to boil over, until the vegetables are cooked through.

With a slotted spoon, remove the vegetables from the stock and put them into a food processor or blender. Add 1/2 cup of the hot stock to the vegetables in the blender and puree until smooth. Then add the purée back into the hot stock and stir to form a thick soup. Season with salt and pepper, and a dash of nutmeg. remember, if you used canned stock, you may not need too much salt.

Enjoy as a first course, or a light dinner with warm bread and a glass of Windsor Cabernet Sauvignon.

Windsor Vineyards

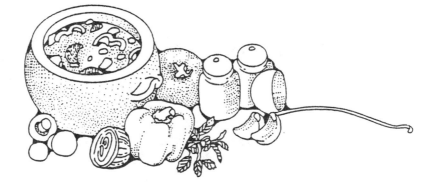

Mushroom Bisque

1 pound mushrooms, ground or minced
1 1/2 cups cream
6 ounces clam juice (1 small bottle)
2 tablespoons minced shallot
6 fennel seeds

3 cups chicken stock
1/4 teaspoon salt
A few grates of nutmeg
4 tablespoons butter
4 tablespoons flour
2 tablespoons dry sherry

A meat grinder produces the best possible texture for the mushrooms, smooth, yet with some interest. The next best alternative is to chop them very finely with a knife. The next easiest alternative is to use a food process, but don't over process.

Bring the mushrooms, cream, clam juice, minced shallots and fennel seeds to a boil and then simmer for 10 minutes.

While the mushrooms are cooking, make a roux by melting the butter, allowing the foam to subside, and then stirring in the flour. Cook this mixture over low heat for 5 minutes, stirring frequently. Set aside to cool.

After the mushrooms have simmered 10 minutes, add the chicken stock, salt and nutmeg.

Add a cup or so of this mixture to the cooled roux, stir smooth, then whisk back into the soup. Bring it up to a simmer and cook for 15 minutes.

Serve garnished with sprigs of fennel or anise, or a sprinkling of chopped hazelnuts. Yields 6 1/2 cups, serves 6.

The idea of using clam juice in a mushroom soup came from Chef Michael Mueller at Portland, Oregon's "2601 Vaughn". Rumor hath it that the idea originated with David Narsai of Berkeley, California's "Narsai's". Then it became mine, and now it's yours. So it goes.

Chef Robert Engel & Christine Topolos
Russian River Vineyards Restaurant

Chilled Cucumber Soup

2 cups chicken stock
3 cucumbers, peeled, seeded and
 sliced
1 tablespoon chopped onion
1 teaspoon snipped fresh dill (or
 use 1/2 teaspoon dried)
Salt and freshly ground pepper

2 cups plain yogurt
1/2 cup finely chopped
 walnuts
Thin slices of unpeeled
 cucumber and snipped fresh
 dill for garnish

In a 4-quart saucepan, combine stock, cucumbers and onion. Bring to a boil; reduce heat and simmer until cucumbers are just tender, about 5 to 7 minutes. Cool.

In a food processor or blender, puree soup, dill, salt and pepper until smooth (in batches if necessary). Add yogurt and walnuts. Chill and adjust seasonings.

Serve cold, garnished with paper-thin slices of cucumber and snipped fresh dill. Serves 8.

Perry Creek Sauvignon Blanc would be a delight with this delicate soup.

Alice Chazen, Owner
Perry Creek Vineyards

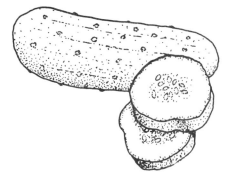

SALADS

Shredded Salt Cod Salad with Tomatoes, Peppers and Onions
(Esqueixada)

1 pound boneless dried salt cod
1 small red (yellow or green) bell
pepper, seeded and sliced into
thin rings
1/2 large red onion, thinly sliced
and separated into rings
1 large ripe tomato, unpeeled and
thinly sliced
3/4 cup extra virgin olive oil

1/4 cup red wine vinegar
4 large garlic cloves, minced
1/2 teaspoon freshly ground
 black pepper, or to taste
Salt to taste, if necessary

AS A GARNISH:
2 ounces black unpitted olives
2 hard-boiled eggs, quartered

Cover salt cod with abundant cold water and soak for 48 hours, changing water 5 or 6 times. Drain and press salt cod with your hands to remove excess water. Discard any skin or bones. With your fingers, shred cod into thin strips.

In a salad bowl, toss shredded salt cod with pepper, onion and tomato. In a small bowl, combine oil, vinegar, garlic and black pepper, beating to blend well. Pour over the salad and, with your hands, toss to coat salt cod and vegetables. Taste for seasoning.

Arrange on a platter or in a bowl and garnish attractively with olives and hard-boiled eggs. Serves 6 to 8.

Esqueixada is a staple on menus of country-style Catalan restaurants, especially in the summertime.

Serve with California Marimar Torres Estate Vineyard Chardonnay.

Marimar Torres

Marimar Torres, President of Torres Wines North America, and of the Torres Vineyard and Winery here in California, is also the author of two cookbooks, "The Spanish Table," and "The Catalan Country Kitchen." Her heritage in wines comes from her family who have been growers and vintners In Spain since the seventeenth century, Her keen interest in food developed in her first home in Catalunya, the rich, gastronomic region of northeastern Spain, and continues today in her new home in the California Wine Country.

Mediterranean Rice Salad

2/3 cup olive oil
1 medium onion, chopped
3 celery stalks, chopped
1 cup long grain rice (uncooked)
1/2 cup blanched almonds, sliced
2 1/2 cups water
2 tablespoons tomato paste

1/2 cup seedless raisins
2 teaspoons dill
2 tablespoons fresh mint, chopped
Salt and pepper to taste
1 cup Green Hungarian wine

In a large saucepan, lightly saute the onion and celery in olive oil until onion becomes translucent.

Add rice and almonds, stirring constantly until the almonds are lightly browned.

Add water, tomato paste, raisins, dill, mint, salt, pepper and wine. Mix well.

Cover and cook over low heat for 25 to 30 minutes, or until rice is done. Stir occasionally, adding more water if needed.

Chill overnight. Serve the salad garnished with sliced tomatoes or mint leaves, or use as filling for tomatoes or peppers.

Full of flavor, this salad offers a colorful and refreshing alternative to standard pasta and potato-based fare. It also makes a wonderful filling for tomatoes and bell peppers.

Recommended wine: Weibel Green Hungarian.

Diana Weibel
Weibel Vineyards

Asparagus and Red Pepper Salad

1 small red pepper, roasted
Zest of 1 orange, finely grated
1 pound fresh asparagus, ends
 trimmed and stalks peeled
1 1/2 tablespoons sugar
1 tablespoon soy sauce

1 tablespoon sesame oil
5 tablespoons peanut oil
1 tablespoon Chinese rice
 vinegar
1 tablespoon sesame seeds,
 toasted

Cut the roasted pepper lengthwise into 1/8-inch strips. In a pan large enough to hold asparagus spears lying flat, cook asparagus approximately 4 minutes until crisp and tender. Drain well and pat dry. In a small bowl, whisk together orange zest, sugar, soy sauce, sesame oil, peanut oil and Chinese rice vinegar. (Dressing can be prepared ahead of time.)

Arrange asparagus spears on serving plate with tips pointed out in a circular fashion. Lay red pepper in strips over asparagus. Drizzle dressing over plate and refrigerate for at least 4 hours. Serve at room temperature. Sprinkle toasted sesame seeds on top. Serves 4.

Our Sonoma County Fumé Blanc is suggested to enhance this salad.

Rhonda Carano, Co-Owner
Ferrari-Carano Vineyards & Winery

The Carano family divide their time between their home in the California Wine Country and their hotel and casino in Reno, Nevada, The Eldorado. It has achieved international recognition for the fine cuisine of its restaurants.

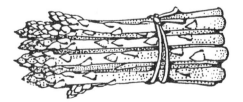

Apple Watercress Salad

1 bunch watercress leaves,
washed and drained
1 stalk celery, sliced thin
1/2 medium red onion, sliced thin
1/4 pound blue cheese, crumbled

2 Granny Smith apples, cored
and cubed
2 tablespoons fresh lemon
juice
1/4 cup olive oil
Salt and pepper to taste

In a small bowl, whisk together lemon juice, oil and pepper and salt to taste. In a large bowl, combine apples, cored and cut into 1/3-inch cubes, watercress, celery, onion and blue cheese, Toss with dressing and season with salt and pepper. Serves 4.

Serve with Kunde Estate Chardonnay.

**Pat Roney, President
Kunde Estate Winery**

Spinach & Cottage Cheese Salad
with Raspberry & Mustard Vinaigrette

1/3 cup red raspberry vinegar
1/3 cup pure olive oil or California
avocado oil
1 tablespoon soy sauce
2 large cloves fresh garlic, pressed
1 bunch fresh spinach, washed
and drained, stems removed

Fresh ground pepper to taste
1/4 cup sweet-n-hot mustard
1 pint small curd cottage
cheese, rinsed and drained
1 basket ripe cherry tomatoes,
washed and stems removed
Salt

Mix together red raspberry vinegar, oil, mustard, soy sauce, garlic, salt and pepper until well blended. Place spinach in large salad bowl and arrange cherry tomatoes around the edge of the bowl. Sprinkle cottage cheese in center. Pour desired amount of dressing over salad. Toss until blended. Serve immediately. Makes 4 to 6 servings.

**Carmen Kozlowski
Kozlowski Farms**

Orzo and Spinach Salad

3/4 pound orzo (Greek rice-shaped pasta)
2 tablespoons olive oil
1/2 cup olive oil
3 tablespoons wine vinegar
3 tablespoons lemon juice
1 teaspoon salt
1/2 teaspoon freshly ground pepper
1 teaspoon Dijon mustard
1 small clove garlic, minced
Pinch thyme
3 tablespoons feta cheese, crumbled
1/2 teaspoon dried oregano
1/4 teaspoon ground cumin
1 bunch spinach, washed, in bite-size pieces
3 tablespoons toasted pine nuts
1/2 cup pitted Kalamata olives, slivered*
1 sweet red pepper, chopped
1/4 cup minced scallions (green and white)
2 teaspoons capers, rinsed and drained

Cook the orzo according to package directions to al dente, drain, run under cold water to stop cooking, then drain thoroughly. Toss with 2 tablespoons olive oil. Prepare the dressing by combining the remaining olive oil with lemon juice, vinegar, herbs and spices, whisking until smooth.

Place the orzo in a large bowl and toss with the dressing. Add spinach, olives, red pepper, scallions and capers and toss to combine. (Can be held, refrigerated, at this point for several hours.) At serving time, add crumbled feta cheese and garnish with toasted pine nuts. Serves 6 to 8.

*Ripe black olives may be substituted for Kalamata, if necessary. The addition of 3/4 pound tiny cooked shrimp makes this into a very nice entre salad.

Mary Evely, Chef
Simi Winery

Chicken Curry Salad

2 chicken breasts, skinned, boned
1/2 teaspoon onion, diced
1/2 teaspoon thyme
1 can water chestnuts, drained and
 coarsely chopped
1/2 can sliced palm hearts, drained
3/4 cup of sugar-roasted peanuts
 and cashews, coarsely chopped
1/2 cup mayonnaise

1/4 cup orange juice
1 teaspoon curry powder
1 small box of fried onion
 rings
1 cup fried chow mein
 noodles
1/2 cup water
1/2 cup white wine
1/2 teaspoon salt

Bring water, wine, thyme, onion and salt to a boil. Add chicken breast, cover pan and simmer very slowly for 30 minutes. Lift off heat and let cook in the broth. (To microwave: bring broth to a boil, add chicken breast and cover. Cook 10 to 12 minutes on medium-low and let cook in broth.) Cut chicken breasts into bite-size pieces.

In a large bowl, mix in mayonnaise, orange juice and curry thoroughly. Add all other ingredients (including chicken) except onion rings and noodles, and mix until everything is coated with the mayonnaise. Just before serving, mix in onion rings and noodles. Serves 6.

Serve with Louis Martini Chardonnay.

Louis M. Martini Winery

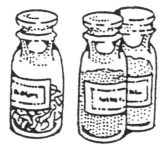

Sonoma Cheese and Chicken Salad
with Mixed Greens
Served with Walnut Dill Vinaigrette

2 large chicken breasts, halved
1 cup shredded jack cheese
1 medium red bell pepper,
 chopped fine
2 tablespoons chopped scallions
2 tablespoons butter
2 tablespoons cooking oil
2 cloves of garlic

Salt and pepper to taste
8 cups mixed greens,
 including arugala, endive,
 chicory and raddichio
1 cup halved toasted walnuts
 (toast & slightly brown on
 cookie sheet approximately
 10 minutes, 400 degree oven)

Heat oven to 350 degrees. Cut a pocket in each chicken breast with a sharp knife, working horizontally from the thickest part of the breast down. Stuff each breast with a mixture of the cheese, pepper and scallion. Saute garlic cloves in oil/butter until golden and remove. Brown chicken breasts on each side on medium-high heat and then bake in oven for 20 to 25 minutes until cooked. Let cool. Cut on diagonal into 8 ribbon slices. Divide greens onto 4 plates. Using spatula, lift chicken ribbons and place on greens. Drizzle vinaigrette over each plate and garnish with walnuts. Serves 4.

WALNUT DILL VINAIGRETTE:

1 tablespoon Dijon mustard
1/4 cup rice vinegar
1/4 cup walnut oil
1/2 cup good quality salad oil

1 inch peeled fresh ginger
1 teaspoon dill weed
Salt and pepper to taste
1/2 teaspoon white sugar

In a food processor, finely chop garlic and ginger. Add mustard, vinegar, sugar, salt, pepper and dill. With machine running, slowly add walnut oil and then cooking oil in steady stream until emulsified.

Serve with a dry white wine.

Sonoma Cheese Factory

Cous Cous Salad

2 tablespoons olive oil
1 1/2 cup cous cous
2 cups chicken broth
1/4 teaspoon pepper

1/4 teaspoon allspice
1/4 teaspoon mace
2 tablespoons butter

TO PREPARE COUS COUS:

Brown cous cous in olive oil in medium skillet. Add broth and seasonings. Stir over medium heat until most of the moisture disappears. Cover and steam for about 5 minutes.

Cooked cous cous - hot
3/4 cup chopped canned tomatoes
 and juice
1 clove garlic, crushed
1/4 teaspoon salt
1/4 cup Parmesan cheese
1 teaspoon Dijon mustard
1/4 cup olive oil

Juice of 1 lemon
Freshly ground pepper to taste
3 green onions, thinly sliced
2 tablespoons chopped fresh
 basil
2 cups chopped spinach, if
 desired

TO PREPARE SALAD:

Combine tomatoes and cous cous and toss lightly. Mash garlic and combine with salt, cheese, mustard, olive oil, lemon juice and pepper. Pour over cous cous and blend in, along with onion, basil and spinach. Serve at room temperature. Serves 5.

Serve with Chardonnay or Fumé Blanc.

Madelene Lyon, Consulting Chef
Konocti Winery

Mediterranean Chicken Salad

4 chicken breasts, skinless, boneless
1 tablespoon chopped shallots
1/2 cup olive oil
2 teaspoons fresh thyme, finely chopped (or 1 teaspoon dried)
3 teaspoons fresh parsley, chopped fine
Juice of 1/2 medium lemon (1/4 cup)

3/4 cup pitted small black olives (preferably Kalamata)
2 tablespoons capers
10 cherry tomatoes, quartered
1/4 pound fresh cooked, pencil thin asparagus, cut in lengths of 1-inch (al dente and still bright green)
1/2 teaspoon fresh ground black pepper

Season chicken breasts lightly with salt and pepper and bake in a 375 degree oven for 15 minutes. Tear chicken into strips or cut into pieces. Toss with olive oil, herbs, lemon juice, capers and shallots. Mix with asparagus, tomatoes and olives. Serve on lettuce leaves or toast points. Serves 8 as hors d'oeuvres or 4 for lunch.

Serve with Robert Mondavi Fumé Blanc Reserve.

**Annie Roberts, Chef, The Vineyard Room
Robert Mondavi Winery**

Annie Roberts learned her profession from her mother, Margrit Biever, Vice President of Cultural Affairs of the Robert Mondavi Winery, who she assisted with luncheons and dinners in The Vineyard Room. She became the Head Chef in 1977. Her approach and style are based upon "simple and tasty" recipes. In 1980, she worked with the chef and staff at Chateau Mouton Rothschild in France, and has, over the years, assisted some of the world's most renowned chefs in the Robert Mondavi Great Chefs Series.

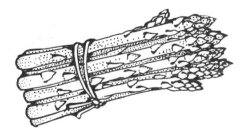

Dilly Pea Salad

16 ounces frozen petite peas
1/3 cup sour cream
1/4 cup mayonnaise
1 tablespoon fresh dill, or 1
teaspoon dry dill, chopped

1 tablespoon fresh parsley,
chopped
5 slices bacon, cooked crisp
and crumbled

Frozen peas may be rinsed with hot water in a sieve for immediate use or simply mixed with remaining ingredients and held at room temperature until thawed. Refrigerate once thawed if not serving immediately.

This is very convenient for large parties because multiple recipes can be made early in the day, placed in a covered casserole dish in an out of the way place and left until party time without needing space in a refrigerator. Serves 4 to 6.

Serve with Quivira Sauvignon Blanc.

Holly P. Wendt, Proprietor
Quivira Vineyards

Turkey Fruit Salad

4 cups chopped cooked turkey
1 cup chopped apple
1 cup chopped walnuts
1 cup seedless grapes

1 cup pineapple tidbits
1/2 cup mayonnaise
1 teaspoon curry powder
1 tablespoon lemon juice

Cut turkey and apple into 1-inch pieces. Place turkey and all fruit into a large bowl. In a small bowl, mix the curry powder, mayonnaise and lemon juice thoroughly. Add to the turkey and fruit and refrigerate for at least 1 hour before serving. Serves 6 to 8 persons. Maraschino cherries can be added for color.

A crispy delicious salad that can be prepared ahead and is excellent for entertaining. VMH

Summer Tomato Salad with Baby Garlic, Basil, Anchovies and Roasted Torpedo Onions

1 large or 4 small red torpedo onions (can use regular red onions)
4 large beefsteak tomatoes
8 cherry tomatoes
8 yellow plum tomatoes
1/4 bunch basil

1 clove garlic, peeled
8 anchovy fillets
Salt and fresh ground black pepper
Vinaigrette dressing (recipe follows)
One loaf quality bakery bread

VINAIGRETTE:

1/4 cup olive oil (plus some to brush bread with)
1 tablespoon sherry wine vinegar

1 clove young or baby garlic, sliced (can use regular garlic)
Salt and fresh ground black pepper to taste

Slice the peeled garlic and add to the vinegar. Whisk in the olive oil. Season if it is not sharp enough. There should be a good balance between oil and vinegar. You should be able to taste both.

Cut large onions into quarters or small onions in halves (keeping skins on). Mix in a bowl with half the vinaigrette. Lightly salt and pepper. Roast in a 350 degree oven for approximately 10 minutes. The onions should still be crunchy, but should be able to be pierced easily with a knife. Take the peel and core off of the onions. Reserve.

Take the core out of the beefsteak tomatoes. Slice each into 4 thick slices. Place down in middle of each plate. Lightly salt and pepper. Mix the cherry and plum tomatoes with the onions and one half of the remaining vinaigrette. Place on either side of the beefsteak tomatoes. Lay the anchovy fillets (2 per plate) across the beefsteak tomatoes on an angle. Dress the beefsteak tomatoes with the remaining dressing.

Slice the basil leaves and sprinkle over the whole plate. Slice the bread approximately 1/4-inch thick. Brush one side of the slices with olive oil and grill or toast until golden brown. Rub with the peeled clove of garlic. Tear in half and place at 4 and 10 o'clock on the plate. Serves 4. Serve with Wente Bros. Sauvignon Blanc.

Kimball Jones, Executive Chef
Wente Bros. Wine Cellars & Restaurant

Fiesta Winter Salad

1 large head Romaine lettuce, torn into bite-size pieces
1 medium size red onion, thinly sliced into rings
1 8-ounce can of mandarin oranges, drained
1 large avocado, sliced and cut into bite-size pieces

Combine all the above, but the avocado, in a large salad bowl. Chill until ready to serve and add avocado and dressing. Serves 6.

DRESSING:

1 tablespoon Dijon type mustard	1 teaspoon tarragon leaves, or
1 tablespoon wine vinegar	2 tablespoons toasted sesame
1/2 cup olive oil	seeds
	Salt and pepper to taste

Combine all the above ingredients.

Serve with St. Clement 1992 Sauvignon Blanc.

St. Clement Vineyards

Parsley Asiago Salad

2 bunches parsley, chopped	3 tablespoons raspberry
1/4 cup Asiago cheese, grated	vinegar
Salt and pepper	1/4 cup olive oil

Combine above ingredients, toss to coat well, season to taste.

Garnish: smoked ham or smoked turkey, or hard boiled eggs cut into wedges, or tomato slices, or red onion, thinly sliced.

Linda Hagen, Executive Chef
Chateau St. Jean

Thai Chicken Salad

SALAD:

4 cups bite-size chicken pieces, roasted or grilled
1 cup bean sprouts
1/2 English cucumber, cut in thin strips
1 stalk celery, chopped

1/2 yellow pepper, chopped

GARNISH:
1/4 cup dry roasted unsalted peanuts, coarsely chopped
6 whole mint leaves

DRESSING:

Juice of 1 lime
1/4 cup fish sauce*
2 tablespoons soy sauce
1 tablespoon sesame oil
1/4 cup light brown sugar
2 serrano chilies, seeded and minced

1/4 teaspoon grated nutmeg
1 tablespoon minced fresh ginger
1/4 cup minced mint leaves
3 tablespoons minced basil leaves

*Available in specialty or oriental markets.

In a medium bowl, whisk together dressing ingredients.

In a large bowl, combine salad ingredients. Add dressing to salad and toss well.

Arrange onto six chilled salad plates. Sprinkle with peanuts. Garnish with mint leaves. Serves 6.

Suggested wine: V. Sattui Off Dry Johannisberg Reisling or V. Sattui Gamay Rouge.

**Robert O'Malley, Operations Manager
V. Sattui Winery**

Peju Province Pasta Salad

1/2 pound pasta, cooked (fusilli or shells)
1/3 pound dry Italian salami
2 red bell peppers
1 green bell pepper
8 carrots
1 red onion

1 bunch green onions with tops
Small chunks of asiago and cheddar cheese (approx. 1/4 pound)
1-2 avocados, sliced and sprinkled with lemon juice *

SEASONING.

Oil, vinegar, and salt to taste
2 tablespoons regular mustard (or more to taste)
Pepper (fresh cracked if possible)

Tarragon (fresh, chopped)
4 tablespoons milk
1/4 cup French Columbard (optional)

Slice all vegetables and the salami into thin bite-sized pieces (julienne style). Combine with pasta, cheese and seasoning. Mix well. Best if prepared one day ahead.   Serves 6 to 8.

* Prepare avocado just before serving salad to prevent discoloring.

Herta Peju, Owner
Peju Province Winery

PASTAS
AND
GRAINS

Butternut Squash and Goat Cheese Agnolotti in a Sage Beurre Blanc Sauce

AGNOLOTTI:

1 large butternut squash
Goat cheese (2 ounces of cheese
 per cup of processed squash)
Salt and pepper to taste

Egg roll wrappers (available in
 most better markets' produce
 section)

For agnolotti filling, place whole squash on baking pan and roast for 1 1/4 hours or until tender. Remove from oven and let cool for 1 hour. Cut in half, remove seeds and scoop out pulp. For every cup of squash, add 2 ounces goat cheese. Place squash and goat cheese in food processor and blend, adding salt and pepper to taste. Remove and chill in refrigerator for 2 hours.

For making agnolotti at home, lay out 6 egg roll skins, lightly coat with egg wash and place one teaspoon of filling in middle of wrapper. Fold in half and gently press air out and seal all sides. With a 3-inch round pastry cutter, cut into half-moon shapes and place on pan covered with cornmeal. You may stack by sprinkling with cornmeal and placing a piece of wax paper between layers. Place in freezer. . . yield approximately 50 agnolotti. (To cook agnolotti, take from freezer to boiling water and cook for about 4 minutes.)

SAUCE:

2 shallots, minced
2 tablespoons butter
2 tablespoons sage, chopped fine

2 cups Chardonnay
1/2 pound butter
Salt and pepper to taste

Mince shallots and saute in 2 tablespoons of butter until translucent. Add finely chopped sage and chardonnay. Reduce by 3/4 to 1/2 cup of liquid. Next, add 1/2 pound butter which has first been cut into small pieces a little at a time, constantly shaking pan in a back-and-forth motion. Finish with salt and white pepper to taste. Serve immediately over agnolotti.

Serve with Cuvaison 1990 Chardonnay.

Cuvaison Winery

Manicotti

1 cup chard or spinach, cooked,
  well drained and chopped
1 cup cottage cheese
1/2 cup Parmesan cheese, grated
1 egg
1 garlic bud, sliced

1 tablespoon basil or parsley,
  chopped
1/2 teaspoon salt
1/4 teaspoon pepper
1 package manicotti

Mix well, stuff uncooked manicotti and place in buttered baking dish in single layer, leaving space to allow for expansion during baking. Cover with the following sauce.

SAUCE:

1 pound ground chuck, browned
1/2 pound pork sausage, browned
1 medium onion, chopped
1 teaspoon salt
1/8 teaspoon pepper
1 4-ounce can sliced mushrooms,
  undrained

1 teaspoon Italian herbs
1/2 cup Zinfandel
1 30-ounce can solid pack
  tomatoes
1 6-ounce can tomato paste

To browned meat mixture, add onion, seasonings and Zinfandel. Simmer until flavors are well blended. Cover manicotti with sauce, sprinkle with Parmesan cheese. Cover with foil and bake for 1 to 1 1/4 hours in oven at 375 degrees.

Serve with Sausal Zinfandel or Cabernet Sauvignon.

Cindy Martin & Roselee Demonstene, Co-Owners
Sausal Winery

A Very Different Wine Country Pasta Dish

1 pound of spinach
1 cup of sliced almonds
1/2 pound of sliced bacon
2 cups of dry short tube pasta
2 cloves of garlic, finely minced
1/2 teaspoon crushed dried red
 pepper

1/4 cup freshly chopped basil
1 tablespoon Dijon mustard
3 tablespoons wine vinegar
2 cups of grated Sonoma Dry
Jack Cheese

Wash and drain the greens, removing and discarding the stems. In a large frying pan over medium heat, toast the almonds until they are slightly brown, about 4 minutes. Remove from pan and put aside. Cook the bacon until it is crisp, then remove from pan, drain, and crumble it.

For the pasta, place in boiling, salted water in large pot, and cook uncovered until tender, but still firm.

While the pasta cooks, discard all but 6 tablespoons of the bacon fat from the frying pan, and add the garlic and pepper, and then the greens. Stir over medium heat until tender. Put the Dijon mustard and wine vinegar into a large bowl, and then mix in the drained pasta, and then the grated cheese, the greens and bacon and chopped basil. Sprinkle the nuts on top. Serves 4 to 6.

Serve with Christian Brothers White Zinfandel 1991.

Greystone Cellars

Sylvia Sebastiani's Spaghetti Sauce

1 pound ground beef (optional)
4 tablespoons olive oil
4 tablespoons butter
4 stalks celery, chopped
4 onions, chopped
4 cloves garlic, chopped fine
1/4 teaspoon rosemary
1/2 cup dried Italian mushrooms, soaked in 1 cup hot water, then chopped

1 large can solid pack tomatoes mashed with liquid
6 8-ounce cans tomato sauce
1 1/2 cups water
1 cup Chablis
1 teaspoon sugar
1/4 teaspoon thyme
1/2 cup parsley, chopped fine
Salt and pepper to taste

If using meat, brown meat in olive oil and butter. Add celery and onions until brown, then add garlic. Salt and pepper to taste; then add spices, mushrooms with their liquid, tomatoes and tomato sauce. Rinse tomato sauce cans with water and add to sauce along with wine and sugar. Cook for 3 hours over low heat, stirring occasionally. If not using meat, start by browning onions and celery and proceed as above. Instead of ground meat, a piece of pot roast can be used.

Brown on all sides, proceed as above letting meat simmer in sauce. After 2 hours, remove meat from sauce and keep warm. Slice and serve as meat course for your dinner. If your family likes their sauce hot, add a small chili pepper, chopped very fine, while sauce is simmering.

This recipe yields a quantity of sauce greater than you would normally use at one time. Freeze the remainder in pint jars, filling 3/4 full. I always keep a supply of frozen sauce on hand - it helps put together numerous meals in a short time.

PASTA COOKING HINT: When boiling pasta, add one teaspoon salt for every 4 cups of water. Also, add one tablespoon of oil so pasta will not stick together while cooking.

Suggested wine: Sebastiani Barbera

Sylvia Sebastiani
Sebastiani Vineyards

Bow Tie Pasta With Wild Mushrooms, Fresh Herbs and a Rich Broth

1 pound wild mushrooms; shiitakes, morels, chantrelles, etc.
1 cup rich chicken broth or bouillon
1 cup rich mushroom stock*
1 tablespoon shallots, chopped
1 tablespoon garlic, chopped
1 tablespoon fresh chopped basil (or 1 teaspoon dried)
1 tablespoon fresh thyme leaves (or 1 teaspoon dried)
1 tablespoon fresh chopped parsley (or 1 teaspoon dried)
4 cups pre-cooked bow tie pasta
Salt and freshly cracked black pepper
1 cup grated Parmesan cheese

Thinly slice the mushrooms and set aside. Combine the 2 broths and add the shallots and garlic. Bring to a boil and reduce to a simmer. Simmer for 5 minutes and add the herbs and pasta. Cook together until pasta is hot.

Season with salt and pepper and serve immediately in bowls with some of the broth ladled over the top. Sprinkle each with a generous amount of Parmesan cheese. Garnish with more of the chopped or whole herbs.

* To make a mushroom stock, use the stems from the various mushrooms along with shallots, garlic, onions, celery, bay and thyme. Place all these ingredients in a sauce pan and cover with water or chicken stock. Bring to boil and simmer for at least 30 minutes. You may also add the water used to reconstitute dried mushrooms if you desire.

Serves 4 as an entree or 6-8 as an Appetizer. Preparation time is 10 to 15 minutes.

Serve with Inglenook-Napa Valley, Estate Bottled Charbono.

Jamie Morningstar
Inglenook-Napa Valley

Ravioli Fritti Filled with Corn and Basil

1 cup fresh or frozen corn kernels	1/2 teaspoon salt
1 clove garlic, chopped	1/2 cup ricotta cheese
1 tablespoon fresh basil, chopped	2 tablespoons finely grated
1 tablespoon butter	Parmigiana
1/4 cup milk	Fresh ground black pepper

Combine corn, garlic and basil in the bowl of a food processor and process until corn is chopped quite small, but do not puree. Combine with milk, butter and salt in a small heavy saucepan. Bring to boil, lower heat and simmer 3 to 4 minutes or longer until very thick. Add the ricotta and stir over high heat for another minute or so to evaporate some of the moisture. Add Parmigiana and a little fresh ground pepper. Taste and add salt as necessary. Chill the mixture well before filling the ravioli.

PASTA DOUGH:

2 large eggs
1 1/4 cup all purpose flour
1 teaspoon salt

Combine all ingredients in a food processor and process until the dough just begins to hold together. Transfer to a lightly floured board and knead by hand until the dough is soft and supple, incorporating more flour if necessary. Pasta dough for ravioli should be quite softer than that for noodles, but not wet or sticky. Let dough rest, covered for at least 1/2 hour before rolling.

Roll out dough in your pasta machine on the next-to-last setting. Place rounded spoonfuls of filling on the lower half of the dough, fold dough over, press dough down around filling. Ravioli should be about 1 1/2 inches square. Cut ravioli with fluted wheel (or sharp knife if you don't have one) leaving very little border around the filling. Press edges together well or the ravioli will break open while cooking. If your dough is nice and moist and not floured excessively, it should stick together with no problem. If not, you may need to moisten the edges with a little water before pressing together.

Place the ravioli on a floured baking sheet and turn occasionally to prevent sticking. Once they are dry enough to not stick, cover them with a towel. They can be made an hour or two in advance of cooking.

COOKING: Add your favorite cooking oil to a skillet to a depth of at least 1 1/2 inches. Heat to 350 degrees. Add as many ravioli as the pan will hold without crowding and fry until nicely browned on each side. Transfer to absorbent paper. Keep in a warm oven while frying subsequent batches. Serve on a tray or platter. Don't mound the ravioli or the moist filling may make ravioli soggy. Yield: about 32 ravioli.

*Notes: If you're not experienced at making your own pasta dough, or would rather not bother, you can purchase sheets of dough from markets or delicatessens that sell fresh pasta noodles. It is really important that fried ravioli be well filled. Boiled ravioli are served in a sauce so that the pasta is flavored both inside and out; fried ravioli are only flavored on the inside.

Suggested wine: Sterling Vineyards 1989 Estate Chardonnay.

Richard Alexei, Food & Wine Consultant
Sterling Vineyards

Penne Pasta with Tomatoes, Herbs and Gorgonzola Cheese

4 teaspoons olive oil
1 large onion, diced
4 large garlic cloves, minced
1 28-ounce can of diced tomatoes
Salt and freshly ground pepper to taste
1 pound penne pasta, cooked as directed on package

8 ounces gorgonzola cheese; one half crumbled finely, one half crumbled into larger pieces
1/2 cup chopped herbs (in winter use a mixture of sage, parsley, thyme and rosemary; in summer try fresh basil leaves)

Saute diced onion in olive oil over medium-high heat until translucent. Add the garlic and saute one minute longer.

Add canned tomatoes to onion-garlic mixture and cook until most of the tomato juices reduce (8 to 10 minutes). Then add salt and pepper to taste and reduce heat to low.

Add crumbled gorgonzola to onion-tomato mixture and stir until the tomato sauce has become somewhat creamy. Pour the tomato sauce over the hot cooked pasta and sprinkle with the chopped fresh herbs.

In summer, use 4 to 6 peeled, seeded and diced golden tomatoes. Serves 4 to 6.

Serve with 1988 Carneros Pinot Noir.

Kristine Schug
Schug Carneros Estate Winery

Wild Boar Lasagne

1 pound ground wild boar or lean
 pork sausage
2-4 large red onions, minced
1 clove garlic, minced
1/2 pound mushrooms, chopped
1/2 cup Cabernet Sauvignon
1 8-ounce can tomato sauce
1 16-ounce can stewed tomatoes
1 8-ounce can tomato paste
1 teaspoon oregano
Pinch of thyme
Pinch of tarragon

Pinch of rosemary
Water as needed
Salt to taste
1 pound lasagne noodles or
 other wide noodles
Salt and pepper to taste
1 cup grated cheddar cheese
1 cup grated Monterey jack or
 other mild white cheese
1/2-1 cup grated Parmesan
cheese

Saute ground boar or sausage in saucepan; add olive oil if meat is so lean it sticks to the pan. Add onions and garlic and saute until transparent. Add mushrooms, Cabernet Sauvignon, tomato sauce, stewed tomatoes, half a can of tomato paste and herbs. Cover and simmer on low heat until pork is cooked and sauce has thickened.

Heat water in a large pot. Add a little salt. When water is at a rolling boil, add lasagne noodles. Cook until soft but still al dente, following package directions. Add remaining tomato paste to wild boar sauce. Season with salt and pepper. Sauce should be thick enough to layer with noodles and cheese.

Layer noodles, sauce, cheddar and Monterey jack cheese alternately in a 13 by 9 by 2 inch baking pan. Finish top layer with grated Parmesan. Bake at 400 degrees for 20 minutes, until cheese is bubbly and begins to brown. If pre-prepared and cold from the refrigerator, cook at 300 degrees for 20 minutes, then at 400 degrees for 10 minutes. Serves 6 to 8.

Enjoy with Guenoc Cabernet Sauvignon or Merlot.

Note: Lean pork sausage can be substituted for wild boar (which is very lean and range fed). With pork sausage, pour off any excess fat.

Karen Melander-Magoon
Guenoc Winery

Risotto with Italian Sausage and Porcini Mushrooms

1 pound Porcini mushrooms (or brown button)
2 tablespoons olive oil
12 ounces hot Italian sausage
6 ounces bacon, fine dice
1 cup onions, small dice
3 cloves garlic, minced

3 cups Arborio rice
4 cups + 2 cups chicken broth, hot
2 cups heavy cream
1 cup Parmesan cheese, grated
1/4 cup chopped parsley

Saute Porcini mushrooms in olive oil, reserve. Remove sausage from casings and cook with bacon for 3 minutes. Add onions, garlic, and cook 2 minutes. Add rice, stir until well glazed. Mix in 4 cups hot chicken broth, 2 cups heavy cream and Porcini mushrooms. Cook an additional 8 to 10 minutes. Add additional chicken broth as needed. Remove from heat, cover and let stand for several minutes. Salt and pepper to taste. Stir in 2 ounces butter and half the Parmesan cheese. Divide on 6 plates and sprinkle with remaining Parmesan cheese and parsley. Serves 6.

Serve with Cline Cellars Zinfandel.

Deanna Williams, Chef
Cline Cellars

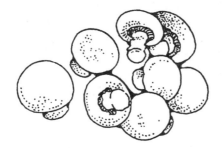

Fettucini with Scallops and Peas
in Saffron Butter Sauce

2 cups shelled fresh peas, or a 10-ounce package of frozen peas.
1 pound fresh fettucini
Court bouillon

1/2 stick unsalted butter, cut into bits and softened
1 1/4 pounds sea scallops
1 cup saffron butter sauce
Parmesan cheese

In a saucepan of boiling salted water, cook the fresh peas until tender, drain well. Cook the pasta in a large pot of boiling water until al dente. Drain and transfer to a large skillet with melted butter in it. Add the peas and salt and pepper to taste and heat the mixture through. Cook your scallops (rinsed, patted dry and any large scallops halved) in a court bouillon broth, drain and add the scallops to the pasta mixture. Add butter saffron sauce and toss with Parmesan cheese. Divide on plates and serve. Serves 6.

SAFFRON BUTTER SAUCE:

1/2 teaspoon crumbled saffron threads
2 tablespoons minced shallots
2 tablespoons white wine vinegar

3 tablespoons dry white wine
3 tablespoons heavy cream
2 sticks cold unsalted butter, cut into pieces

In a small heavy saucepan, combine the saffron, shallots, vinegar and wine, bring to a simmer over moderate heat. Reduce to about 2 tablespoons. Add the cream and simmer, whisking occasionally until reduced to about 2 tablespoons. (Sauce can be prepared up to this point 1 hour in advance and kept covered at room temperature; bring to a simmer before continuing.) Season the mixture with salt and pepper, reduce heat and whisk in butter a piece at a time, lifting pan from the heat occasionally to cool the mixture and adding each new piece of butter before the previous one has completely melted. (The sauce should not be to hot to liquify.) Remove from heat and correct seasoning. Makes about 1 cup.

We serve our Alexander Valley Chardonnay with this entree.

Rhonda Carano, Co-Owner
Ferrari-Carano Vineyards & Winery

Risotto with Three Grains

1/4 pound butter
4 onions, chopped fine
1 carrot, chopped fine
1 1/2 teaspoons quatre-espices*
3 cups Zinfandel
1 quart chicken stock
Bouquet garni
1 cup converted rice

1 cup wild rice
1 cup coarse cracked wheat
1/2 pound fresh mushrooms
 (boleti or chantrelles)
Salt and pepper
2 cloves garlic, minced
Chopped parsley

Heat 2 tablespoons butter, add onions and carrots and saute until onions are golden. Add quatre-espices, wine and broth. Bring to a boil; add bouquet garni and reduce to 6 cups. Remove the bouquet garni but do not strain. Heat 4 tablespoons butter in heavy bottomed pot (cast iron). Add rice; stir until well-coated and lightly browned. Add 2 cups of stock reduction. Cover with paper towel and lid, and cook until done. Heat 4 tablespoons of butter in another pot.

Add wild rice and toss quickly to coat and heat. Add 3 cups of stock reduction, cover and cook until liquid has been absorbed and grains have opened, about 30 minutes. Heat 4 tablespoons of butter in another pot. Add cracked wheat and toss to coat. Add the last cup of stock reduction. Remove from heat and keep covered until all liquid has been absorbed. Heat last 2 tablespoons of butter in saucepan. Add sliced mushrooms. Add salt and pepper, and saute until all juices run out of mushrooms. Add juices to the cracked wheat. Continue sauteing the mushrooms until golden. Mix mushrooms with all grains. Adjust seasoning. Add garlic and parsley. Serves 8 to 12.

*Quatre-Espices: 3/4 teaspoon cinnamon; 2 teaspoons allspice; 1/2 teaspoon ground cloves; 1/2 teaspoon ground cardamon; 3/4 teaspoon grated nutmeg; 2 teaspoons coriander.

Serve with 1989 De Loach Vineyards Estate Bottled Zinfandel.

Christine De Loach
De Loach Vineyards

"Starmont" Risotto

1 pound Arborio rice
1 onion, chopped
1/2 pound fresh shiitake
 mushrooms, chopped
1/4 cup sundried tomatoes,
 chopped
5 cups homemade vegetable stock
 (or 5 vegetable bouillon cubes in
 5 cups water)
3/4 bottle dry white wine

1/4 cup milk
1/4 cup grated Parmesan
Pinch of saffron
1 tablespoon extra virgin olive
 oil
1 tablespoon unsalted butter
2 cups broccoli, blanched,
 dried and coarsely chopped
 by hand

Heat the olive oil and butter in a large saute pan until hot. Gently saute the onion and mushrooms until the onions are soft and golden brown. In the meantime, combine the milk and Parmesan, stirring thoroughly and set aside.

Add the rice to the onion mixture and continue stirring for approximately 5 minutes until all excess moisture has been absorbed and the grains of rice are thoroughly coated. Increasing the heat, carefully add the wine and continue stirring until the mixture becomes syrupy. Continue stirring, adding the stock approximately one cup at a time, until all the liquid is absorbed.

Add the milk/cheese mixture together with the broccoli and sundried tomatoes. Cook for several minutes. Turn off the heat and add the saffron, again stirring well. Serve in heated bowls. Four to 6 generous servings.

Serve with Merryvale 1990 "Starmont" Chardonnay.

Robert Levy, Winemaker
Merryvale Vineyards

Sweet and Spicy Zinfandel Sauce
Served Over Chocolate Pasta

1 medium red onion
3 celery ribs, chopped
2 cloves garlic, minced
1/4 cup Italian parsley, chopped
3 medium-sized ripe tomatoes,
 peeled, seeded and chopped
1/2 cup extra light, virgin olive oil
1 pound ground mild Italian
sausage
1 cup Zinfandel
1 28-ounce can crushed pear
tomatoes

1/2 teaspoon ground ginger
1/4 cup fresh ground black
 pepper *
1/2 cup Zinfandel
1/4 cup raisins
3 tablespoons semi-sweet
 chocolate chips
1 tablespoon granulated sugar
1/2 teaspoon ginger
1 teaspoon salt

* Must use fresh ground pepper. If not available, cut pepper in half to 1/8 cup.

Heat the oil in a large saucepan. Add the celery, onion, garlic, tomatoes and parsley. Cook slowly for 15 minutes. Add the ground sausage and allow to saute with the vegetables. Add the cup of wine and simmer for 5 minutes. Add the crushed pear tomatoes and seasonings. Simmer for 25 minutes. Meanwhile, in a small bowl, pour in the 1/2 cup of wine, add the raisins, chocolate chips, sugar and ginger. Allow to rest for 20 minutes. Add this mixture to the sauce and simmer for 5 minutes. Ladle the sauce over the prepared pasta and serve immediately.

CHOCOLATE PASTA:

1 1/2 cups flour
2 large eggs (room temperature)
1 teaspoon vegetable oil

2 1/2 tablespoons cocoa
 powder
Pinch of salt

Mix flour and cocoa powder. Dump onto the work surface. Form into mound and make a well in the center of the flour mound. Break the eggs into the center, beat the eggs with a fork. Add the vegetable oil, mix well. With a fork, start drawing the flour into the egg and oil mixture with a circular motion, using one hand for mixing and the other to support the outside wall of the well. When the liquid is no longer runny, tumble the rest of the flour through the eggs working until crumbly.

Using a scraper, move the combination to one side and scrape work surface clean. Wash and dry hands. Knead dough until smooth, compact and elastic. Cover with damp cloth or a bowl and allow to rest 30 minutes.

Roll out dough, using pasta machine. Cut fettucine noodles.

Chocolate pasta cooking instructions: Add pasta to 4-5 quarts rapidly boiling water, stir to separate. Bring to second boil and cook uncovered 3-5 minutes, stirring occasionally. Drain. Serves 4 to 6.

Serve with Cline Cellars Zinfandel.

Niki Buchler, Cuisine Consultant
Cline Cellars

Cous-Cous (Near East Pasta)

1/2 cup cous-cous
3/4 cup water
2 tablespoons olive oil
1/2 cup snow peas
1/2 cup sliced carrots
1/2 cup chopped red pepper

1 teaspoon chopped fresh
 mint
1 tablespoon chopped parsley
1 tablespoon lemon juice
Salt and pepper to taste

Cook cous-cous according to directions on box using olive oil instead of butter. Remove ends and strings from snow peas, and cook in boiling water to "al dente," about 3 minutes. Drain and rinse in cold water. Clean and slice carrot and cook to "al dente," about 5 minutes in boiling water. Drain well and run cold water over carrots. Combine all ingredients. Let stand in refrigerator approximately 1 hour or until well chilled. If dry, add more French dressing, or olive oil and lemon juice 2 to 1. Serves 6.

Serve with Louis Martini Chardonnay.

Louis M. Martini Winery

Lucy's Tomato Tuna Sauce & Pasta

3/4 to 1 pound tuna filet, 1-inch
 thick
1/4 cup olive oil
2 tablespoons minced onion
1 tablespoon minced garlic
1/2 cup Chardonnay or Pinot Noir
1 tablespoon cream (optional)

1 14 1/2-ounce can cut up
 tomatoes with juice
1 tablespoon drained, rinsed
 capers
2 tablespoons pine nuts
1 tablespoon parsley

Heat olive oil in medium saute pan. Add onion and garlic and saute for 1 minute. Add tuna and wine. Cook about three minutes on each side or until tuna is medium done and will flake into small chunks. Add tomatoes and juice, capers and pine nuts. Simmer until liquid thickens slightly. In the meantime, boil the pasta. While the pasta is cooking, add parsley and cream (if desired) to the sauce. Salt and pepper to taste. Pour over drained pasta and serve hot. Serves 6 as a first course, 4 as a main course.

A note from the chef: A recipe that satisfies red or white wine lovers! This is a versatile dish that pairs equally well with a substantial Chardonnay like Rodney Strong Chalk Hill Chardonnay, or a soft red like the Rodney Strong River East Pinot Noir. Whichever wine you prefer to drink with dinner, use that also in preparing this recipe.

Lucy Cafaro
Rodney Strong Vineyards

MEATS

Stuffed Veal Loin

1 boneless loin of veal with flank attached, weighing about 4 pounds with tenderloin and bones separate
1 egg
1/3 cup bread crumbs from fresh sourdough French bread without crusts
1/4 cup milk
1 leek, finely chopped (white portion only)
1/4 cup chopped parsley
1/2 teaspoon salt
1/4 teaspoon ground pepper

Scrape attached meat off the bone with a spoon. Take these scraps and the chain running along the loin off, and process in a food processor until chopped. Add the egg and process again. Mix bread and milk together and add to meat mixture. Stir in leeks, parsley, garlic, salt and pepper until blended.

Spread mixture on inner surface of veal loin. Cut tenderloin in half lengthwise to make a longer piece to fit the length of the loin. Place tenderloin in the crease between the flank and the loin, roll and tie. Season with salt and pepper, melt 2 tablespoons butter in a large saute pan and brown meat evenly over medium heat. Place meat in a roasting pan and roast in a 400 degree oven for about 45 minutes or until it has an internal temperature of 130 degrees. Turn meat a couple of times during roasting. Let rest about 15 minutes. Remove string and serve. Serves 8.

Serve with Robert Mondavi Pinot Noir Reserve.

**Annie Roberts, Chef, The Vineyard Room
Robert Mondavi Winery**

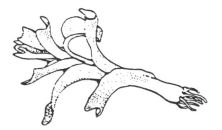

Spirited Ragout

1 pound beef stew meat	1 sweet potato, steamed or blanched
1 pound lamb stew meat	
1 pound pork stew meat	2 turnips, steamed or blanched
2 cups Petite Sirah or Merlot	
3 tablespoons chopped fresh sage	1 small bunch broccoli, steamed or blanched
2 teaspoons ground cumin	
Sprinkle of freshly ground pepper	3 carrots, steamed or blanched
4 tablespoons butter	
3 cloves garlic, minced	2 ounces bittersweet chocolate, chopped
1 teaspoon salt	
1 cup beef stock	

Marinate the meats in the wine, sage, cumin and pepper overnight. Lift meat out of marinade and dry with paper towels. Bring the marinade to a boil and strain. Throw out any solids. Melt butter in a large skillet and add the meat. Cook until browned. Add the garlic and cook 1 minute more. Add the marinade, stock and salt. Simmer about 1 hour or until meat seems tender but not falling apart. Add the chocolate and let melt completely. Add the cooked vegetables and simmer about 15 minutes. Correct seasonings with salt and pepper. Serve over cooked rice (seasoned with a little cumin and butter). Serves 8.

Serve with Martini Merlot or Reserve Petite Sirah.

Louis Martini Winery

This recipe may well become a family favorite of yours, with its combinations of meats, the intermingling of the spices and the wine with the chocolate!

Osso Buco

3 pounds veal shanks, cut into 6 pieces about 2 inches thick
1/2 cup flour
1/4 cup butter
1 tablespoon olive oil
2 teaspoons salt
1/2 teaspoon freshly ground black pepper
1 medium yellow onion, chopped
1/2 cup chopped carrots
1/2 cup chopped celery
1 teaspoon garlic, finely chopped
1/4 teaspoon marjoram
1/4 teaspoon thyme
1 teaspoon lemon rind, grated
1 teaspoon orange rind, grated
2 anchovy filets, mashed
1 cup dry white wine
1 cup tomato pulp
2 cups chicken stock
1/2 cup parsley, finely chopped
1 bay leaf
1/2 cup cognac

Ask your butcher to prepare the veal shanks. Roll the shanks in flour and brown on all sides in 3 tablespoons butter and the olive oil. Salt and pepper to taste. Add the onion, carrots, celery, garlic, marjoram, thyme, lemon and orange rind and the anchovy, if desired, and cook over very low heat for approximately 10 minutes, or until the vegetables are soft.

Add the wine and cook until almost completely evaporated. Add tomato pulp and chicken stock, cover and cook over low heat until tender, about 1 1/2 hours. If sauce is evaporating too quickly, add a little chicken broth. Add bay leaf and simmer.

When ready to serve, finish with the remaining butter and cognac and sprinkle with chopped parsley. Serves 6.

We serve our Alexander Valley Cabernet Sauvignon with this.

**Rhonda Carano, Co-Owner
Ferrari-Carano Vineyards & Winery**

Braised Lamb Shanks with Rosemary Dumplings

6 lamb shanks (5 to 6 pounds)
4 ounces butter
1 medium onion, chopped
1 carrot, chopped
1 rib celery, chopped
3 cloves garlic, crushed
1 bay leaf

5 thyme sprigs
8 parsley stems
2-inch piece of rosemary
10 white peppercorns
2 whole cloves
3 cups Cabernet
1 1/2 quarts good veal stock

DUMPLINGS:

GARNISH:

1 cup all purpose flour
1 1/2 teaspoons baking powder
3 teaspoons chopped rosemary
1 beaten egg
1/4 cup milk
Salt and pepper
2 teaspoons melted butter

18 each of turned carrots,
 turnips and button onions
4 ounces peas
6 ounces French beans
10 ounces button mushrooms

Place the lamb shanks with all the ingredients (except the butter and stock) and marinate overnight. Take out the lamb shanks and strain the liquid off, keeping everything. In a large pot, melt the butter, season the lamb with salt and pepper, sear off well in the butter. Remove lamb from the pot and sweat the vegetables, etc., which came from the marinade. Return lamb to the pot with the vegetables, add the stock and the liquid from the marinade, bring to a boil, cover and place in a preheated oven at 325 degrees. This will need to cook about 1 1/2 hours, or until meat is tender.

To make the dumplings, combine flour, baking powder and 1/2 teaspoon each of salt and pepper. Stir in the rosemary. Combine the egg, milk and butter, add to the flour mixture, stir only until it is combined.

The garnish of vegetables should be blanched and ready to add to the broth after it has been strained and reduced.

Check the lamb shanks. You will need to put the dumpling mixture, a tablespoon at a time, directly onto the simmering broth and allow dumplings to cook for 15 minutes. When the shanks are tender and the dumplings are cooked, take the pot from the oven, remove the dumplings and lamb shanks to a warm serving platter and keep warm. Strain broth, pushing some of the flavor from the vegetables through. Reduce the broth to thicken in a saucepan. Reheat the garnish vegetables in the broth, season with salt and pepper. Pour over the lamb shanks and serve. Serves 6.

Recommended wine: Chateau Souverain Cabernet Sauvignon.

Martin W. Courtman, Executive Chef
Chateau Souverain

Martin W. Courtman, Executive Chef at Chateau Souverain, a native of England, received his schooling, first at Harlow College, and then from the City and Guilds of London Institute's Certification Program in food preparation, service, catering and beverages, with honors.

His restaurant experience in the United States includes key positions at The Mansion on Turtle Creek in Dallas, The Carlyle in Houston and, as Executive Chef of the Stanley Hotels in Estes Park, Colorado.

His cuisine features modern, yet simple foods, carefully matched to the wines of Chateau Souverain.

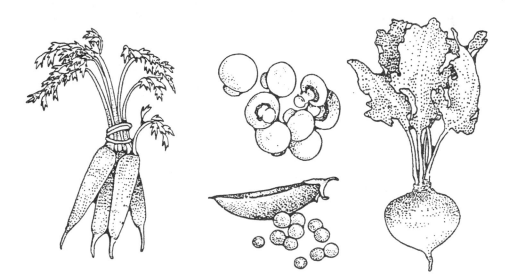

Saltimbocca Alla Roma

12 veal scallopini
12 slices prosciutto, very thin
12 fresh sage leaves

6 tablespoons butter
3/4 cup Chardonnay
Salt and pepper to taste

Layer each scallopini with 1 slice prosciutto and top with 1 sage leaf. Fasten together with a toothpick, by making a "stitch" through the leaf and meats. Melt butter over medium heat in a saute pan. Saute each scallopini for 2 minutes on the veal side, turn and saute for 1 minute on the prosciutto side. Transfer to a heated platter and keep warm. Pour Chardonnay into saute pan and reduce over high heat for 2 minutes. Pour over scallopini and serve, garnished with a fresh sage bouquet. Serves 6.

Serve with Raymond Napa Valley Chardonnay.

Virginia Raymond
Raymond Vineyards and Cellar

A Chardonnay Ham Glaze

3/4 cup grape juice
1/4 cup orange juice
1/2 cup raisins
Zest of 1 chopped lemon
Zest of 1 chopped orange
1 tablespoon cornstarch

1/2 cup Chardonnay
10 chopped dried apricots
1 ounce slivered almonds
Dash of mace
Dash of nutmeg
1/2 tablespoon Dijon mustard

In a sauce pan, simmer wine, grape and orange juice, raisins and zest for 10 minutes until raisins are plumped and liquid starts to reduce. Add almonds and apricots. In a separate bowl, mix cornstarch, mustard and 2 tablespoons cold water. Add slowly 3 tablespoons hot sauce. Mix well and return to pan. Cook, stirring for 1 minute. Add mace and nutmeg to taste. Makes 1 cup. Serve with finished ham.

Jill Davis, Winemaker
Buena Vista-Carneros Estate Winery

Almond Stuffed Pork Tenderloin

2-3 pounds pork tenderloin
Flour
Salt and pepper to taste
1-2 strips bacon
1/2 cup toasted almonds
1/2 cup raisins

Cinnamon
1 teaspoon dry mustard
2 tablespoons oil
1 cup chopped onion
1/2 cup bouillon
1 cup sherry

Make holes 1 inch apart in the top side of the tenderloin. Use a sharp knife, piercing about halfway through the meat. Stuff holes with pieces of bacon, raisins and almonds that have been powdered with cinnamon. Rub tenderloin with salt, pepper and cinnamon. Powder with flour, brown in hot oil in heavy frying pan with a lid.

Place the browned tenderloin in a shallow roasting pan. Add onions, bouillon, sherry and dry mustard. Cover and bake until done, about 45 minutes to 1 hour in oven preheated to 375 degrees. Baste while cooking. Serve with sauce either over meat or apart. Also delicious cold.

Serve with Christian Brothers Napa Valley Cabernet Sauvignon, 1989.

Greystone Cellars

Grilled Tenderloin of Venison
with Cassis Berries

12-16 ounces tenderloin of venison

MARINADE:

4-6 rosemary stalks, washed and cut to 4-5 inches
1/2 bottle red wine (Merlot if available)
1/2 cup chopped each: carrot, celery, onion
Bouquet garni* with few sprigs fresh rosemary added
*(Parsley, thyme and bayleaf)

2 tablespoons mustard
2-3 tablespoons extra virgin olive oil
3-4 tablespoons cassis berries (black currents), lightly crushed
3 tablespoons soy sauce

Mix all ingredients, except rosemary stalks, in glass or stainless steel pan and marinate venison, lightly covered, in refrigerator for 24 to 36 hours, turning occasionally.

SAUCE:

3/4 cup Merlot, reduced to 1/4 cup
1/2 cup veal demi-glace
1/2 cup pork or beef demi-glace
Arrowroot slurry
4-5 tablespoons cassis berries (black currants) with a bit of the juice

Pinch of fresh finely chopped rosemary
Pinch of fresh finely chopped parsley
Salt and pepper
2-3 tablespoons butter

Heat and bring to boil Merlot, veal and pork demi-glace. Thicken with arrowroot. Add cassis berries, adjust thickness if necessary. Add herbs and adjust seasoning. Finish with butter. Keep warm.

ASSEMBLY:

Cut venison into 1 to 1 1/2 inch cubes and thread on presoaked rosemary stalks. Place on preheated grill, 2 to 3 minutes per side. Keep venison rare to medium rare. Lay venison on small bed of fresh rosemary and fried parsley. Pour small amount of sauce over top and serve remaining sauce on side. Serves 4.

Serve with Matanzas Creek Sonoma Valley Merlot.

Sarah Kaswan, Chef
Matanzas Creek Winery

Veal Rolls with Apple Stuffing

12 thin veal scallops (about 1 1/2 pounds)	1 cup chopped onion
1/2 teaspoon poultry seasoning	2 1/2 cups soft bread cubes
2 tablespoons flour	1 cup apple, peeled and coarsely chopped
1 teaspoon salt	6 tablespoons butter
Pepper to taste	3/4 cup Chardonnay

In a large skillet, melt 4 tablespoons butter. Add onions; saute, stirring often until golden, about 5 minutes. Add bread, apple, salt and poultry seasoning. Cook, stirring over medium heat about 4 minutes. Place 1 heaping tablespoon of stuffing on each veal slice, roll up and secure with wooden pick. Roll in flour, salt and pepper. Heat remaining butter in skillet, brown rolls well on all sides. Add wine and simmer, covered, for 30 to 35 minutes or until tender. Remove picks, spoon juices over rolls. Serves 4 to 6.

Serve with Landmark 1990 Sonoma County Chardonnay.

Landmark Vineyards

Peaches Stuffed with Pork and Almonds

6 large almost-ripe peaches, unpeeled
1/3 cup slivered almonds
1/3 cup (2 ounces) ground pork
1/4 cup fresh white bread crumbs
1 egg, slightly beaten
1/4 teaspoon almond extract
Salt and pepper to taste
2 tablespoons olive oil
2 tablespoons butter

1/4 cup all purpose flour
1/4 cup peach brandy
2 cups brown stock or beef consommé (brown stock may be purchased frozen in specialty markets)
1/3 cup Brut Champagne
5 whole cloves
Fresh mint leaves (optional)

Heat oven to 350 degrees. Slice 1/4 inch from stem end of peaches, so peaches will stand upright. With grapefruit knife or melon baller, cut out peach pit, being careful not to cut through bottom or sides. Toast almonds on baking sheet until golden, 15 minutes. Grind in blender or food processor.

Mix almonds, pork, bread crumbs, egg and almond extract thoroughly; season to taste with salt and pepper. Stuff peaches loosely with mixture. In large skillet, heat oil and butter over medium-low heat. Dip stuffed side of peach into flour, fry peaches, stuffed side down, until golden (7 to 10 minutes). Transfer peaches to flameproof casserole; keep warm. Add brandy to skillet, heat to boiling, scraping bottom with wooden spoon. Add ham stock, Champagne and cloves; return to boil. Pour over peaches. Bake until pork is done, 45 minutes. Cover loosely, if necessary, to prevent drying.

Transfer peaches to serving platter, stuffing side up; keep warm. Reduce cooking liquid to 3/4 cup over high heat; taste and adjust seasoning with salt and pepper. Pour reduced liquid over peaches; garnish with mint. Serves 6.

Recommended wine: Gloria Ferrer 1985 Carneros Cuvée.

Gloria Ferrer Champagne Caves

Lamb Chops with Spinach and Mushrooms

8 lamb chops
1/2 teaspoon minced rosemary
1/4 cup olive oil
1 1/2 teaspoons salt
1/2 cup Merlot wine

1 pound shiitake mushrooms, thickly sliced
1 pound spinach, rinsed and stemmed
2 tablespoons unsalted butter

Preheat broiler or barbecue grill. Rub chops with 2 tablespoons olive oil, 1/2 teaspoon salt and 1/4 teaspoon rosemary. Set aside. In large skillet, heat 1 tablespoon olive oil over high heat, add mushrooms, 1/2 teaspoon salt and 1/4 teaspoon rosemary. Cook until caramelized. Set aside. Broil chops about 5 inches from heat until golden on outside, rosy inside, about 3 minutes per side.

Reheat mushrooms, arrange down center of 4 plates, place 2 chops over the mushrooms. Keep warm. In large skillet, heat 1 tablespoon olive oil over medium heat. Add spinach and 1/2 teaspoon salt, cook to wilt. Spoon around chops.

Cover and keep warm. Add wine to spinach juices and cook over high heat until reduced to 1/4 cup. Reduce heat to low and add butter to thicken. Pour over chops and serve. Serves 4.

Gail Paquette, Chef
Belvedere Winery

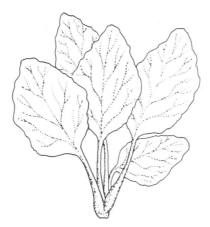

Armenian Lamb Shanks with Pilaf

4 shanks, cleaned and fat trimmed	2 cups chopped onions
4 cloves chopped garlic	2 cups chopped carrots
1 cup catsup	1 cup chopped celery
1 teaspoon Cayenne	1 cup red wine
1 cup chopped red pepper	1/4 cup Worcestershire
1 cup chopped green pepper	1 teaspoon salt
1 leak (white only) sliced	

Put shanks in a large heavy pot (large enough to have lamb shanks in single layer). Mix seasonings and vegetables. Pour over shanks and bake in a low 325 degree oven, covered for 2 to 4 hours. Scoop vegetables and sauce over lamb while cooking. When tender, place one shank on plate with extra sauce. Serve with rice pilaf and string beans. Serves 4.

PILAF:

2/3 cube butter	2 cups water or chicken broth
1/2 cup broken vermicelli	(broth is best)
Salt and pepper	1 cup long grain white rice

Melt butter in heavy skillet. Add vermicelli and stir until light brown. Add rice and stir until all rice is coated. Pour hot chicken both over rice, stirring a few minutes. Bring to a boil and reduce heat to simmer. Add salt and pepper to taste. Cover tightly and simmer for 35 minutes. Remove lid, fluff with fork. Add currants and pine nuts (if desired). Serves 4.

Serve with Adler Fels Sobra Vista or Sangiacomo Chardonnay.

Adler Fels Winery

Adler Fels Winery owner Ayn Ryan Coleman has an Armenian heritage. A descendant of the Merzoian family, who emigrated to California from Bitlis, Armenia five generations ago, she keeps family tradition alive through the preparation of recipes that have been handed down from generation to generation.

Lamb Rack with Hazelnut Crust with a Fig Cabernet Sauce

2 1/2 racks of lamb
1/3 cup hazelnuts, ground
2 tablespoons olive oil
2 tablespoons chopped fresh
 thyme

Salt and pepper to taste
2 tablespoons chopped fresh
 rosemary

Prepare lamb racks. Combine hazelnuts and herbs with oil and press into meat. Season with salt and pepper. Cook racks by sauteing meat side down in olive oil until well browned. Place racks in 400 degree oven and cook for about 15 to 20 minutes. Allow to sit 5 minutes before slicing. While rack is cooking, prepare sauce. Place lamb chops in pool of this sauce on individual plates. Garnish with fresh figs and fresh herbs.

CABERNET AND FIG DEMI-GLACE:

3 shallots, chopped fine
2 cloves garlic, chopped fine
1 cup Cabernet Sauvignon

1 quart strong lamb stock
4 dried figs, coarsely chopped
Salt and pepper to taste

Put shallots and garlic and Cabernet Sauvignon in saucepan and reduce to about 1/4 cup. Add stock and reduce by half. Add figs. Continue to reduce until slightly thickened. Strain and keep warm until lamb is ready.

The wine: Our Alexander Valley Cabernet Sauvignon.

Rhonda Carano, Co-Owner
Ferrari-Carano Vineyards & Winery

Stuffed Roast Veal
with Tarragon and Pinot Noir

4-5 pound boneless veal roast
2 onions, minced
1 cup minced celery
1/2 cup minced parsley
2 tablespoons fresh tarragon
 leaves, minced
3 cloves garlic, minced
3 tablespoons butter

Salt and pepper, to taste
1/2 pound pancetta (Italian
 bacon)
1/2 cup Pinot Noir
1 cup veal or chicken stock
1/2 teaspoon fresh tarragon
 leaves, minced

Cut and pound the veal into an even, oblong shape. Saute the onions and celery until softened, about 3 minutes. Stir in parsley, tarragon (2 tablespoons) and garlic. Salt and pepper to taste. Spread mixture evenly over the veal and roll up, starting at the short side. Tie with string at 2-inch intervals. Lightly pepper the veal. Put slices of pancetta in overlapping layers over the veal.

Roast the meat on a rack until a meat thermometer inserted in the center of the roast registers between 135 to 140 degrees, about 1 1/2 hours.

Remove roast from pan and pour off any fat. Add wine and deglaze, scraping up any brown bits of meat. Bring wine to a boil and cook until reduced to half. Add the stock and remaining tarragon (1/2 teaspoon) and cook over medium-high heat until sauce is reduced to about 1 cup and is just slightly thickened. Serves 6 to 8.

Suggested wine: Rodney Strong Vineyards River East Pinot Noir.

Bea Beasley
for
Rodney Strong Vineyards

Apples and Lamb Chops

4 shoulder blade lamb chops,
 trimmed of fat
8 medium potatoes, thinly sliced
Salt and pepper
1 tablespoon flour
1 1/4-1 1/2 cup bouillon
1/4 cup grated cheese

2 tablespoons butter
4 medium onions, thinly sliced
4 apples, peeled, quartered
 and cooked
1/2 cup Late Harvest
 Gewurztraminer

Brown chops in hot butter. Keep hot on another platter. Cook potatoes and onions in same pan of butter until golden. Place layer of potatoes and onions in buttered baking dish; top with chops and cover with rest of potatoes and onions. Season with salt and pepper. Arrange apples around edge of dish. Sprinkle flour into same pan in which chops were browned. Cook until brown. Pour in bouillon; bring to a boil. Stir constantly. Add Late Harvest Gewurztraminer and pour over chops. Sprinkle with cheese. Bake at 375 degrees for 1 hour or until tender. Serves 4.

Suggested Wine: Mark West 91 Russian River Pinot Noir.

Carolann Heyden
Mark West Winery

Mustard-Grilled Lamb Burgers

1 1/4 pounds extra-lean ground
lamb
1 1/4 cups minced mushrooms
(about 5 ounces)
1/2 cup chopped hazelnuts
(filberts) chopped (about 2 1/2
ounces)
1 clove garlic, minced or pressed

1 egg white, lightly beaten
1 teaspoon salt
1/4 teaspoon black pepper
Vegetable oil for brushing on
grill rack
Mustard
8 hamburger buns, split
Lettuce leaves

Combine the lamb, mushrooms, hazelnuts, garlic, egg white, salt and
pepper in a medium-sized bowl. Divide the meat mixture into 8 equal
portions and shape into round patties. In a grill with a cover, prepare
a medium-hot fire for direct-heat cooking. Brush the grill rack with
vegetable oil. Place the patties on the grill and cook, turning once,
until done to your preference (5 to 8 minutes on each side). After
turning, spread the tops of the patties with mustard. During the last
few minutes of cooking, place the buns, cut side down, on the outer
edges of the grill to toast lightly. Serve the burger and toasted buns
with the Eggplant Salsa, Basil Yogurt and lettuce for guests to
assemble as desired. Serves 8.

EGGPLANT SALSA:

1 large eggplant, sliced crosswise
3/4-inch thick
1/4 cup olive oil
1/2 teaspoon chili powder
1 teaspoon salt
1 teaspoon ground cumin

1/2 small yellow onion,
unpeeled
2 tablespoons diced canned
roasted red pepper
1 tablespoon balsamic vinegar
or red wine vinegar

Brush both sides of each eggplant slice with some of the olive oil.
Combine the chili powder, salt and cumin and sprinkle both sides of
the slices. Brush the grill rack with vegetable oil. Place the eggplant
slices on the grill, cover and cook, turning once, until very brown on
both sides. Meanwhile, brush the onion half with olive oil. Grill,
covered, until the skin is crisp and blackened.

Remove eggplant and onion to a plate to cool. Slip off and discard the
skins from the eggplant and onion, then chop coarsely. In a bowl,
lightly combine the eggplant, onion, red pepper, and vinegar and set
aside.

BASIL YOGURT:

1/2 cup low-fat plain yogurt   1/2 cup sour cream
2 tablespoons chopped fresh basil

Combine the yogurt and basil in a blender or a food processor and blend well. Remove to a bowl and fold in the sour cream. Cover and chill.

Serve Sutter Home Zinfandel with this interesting dish.

Sutter Home Winery

Good lamb recipes, other than the standard chops, roasts, etc., are not easily found, but this one is really good. Good enough to win $3,000 in Sutter Home's National Burger Cook-Off, for 2nd Prize.

Curried Lamb Stew

1/2 cup cooking oil   1 cup Chardonnay
2 pounds lamb stew meat   2 teaspoons salt
1/3 cup flour   1/4 teaspoon pepper
1 tablespoon curry powder   1/8 teaspoon garlic salt
1 cup water   1 onion, thinly sliced

Heat oil in heavy pan. Add meat and brown well. Remove meat from pan. Blend in flour and curry in drippings. Add water and wine and cook, stirring constantly until mixture is thick and smooth. Add salt, pepper and garlic salt. Put meat in pan and top with onion slices. Cover and simmer 1 1/2 hours, or until meat is tender. Serve with rice and a green salad. I usually make this dish early in the day and then chill to remove the top fat. Reheat before serving. Serves 4 to 6.

Wine recommendation: Kunde Estate Chardonnay.

Leslie Kunde
Kunde Estate Winery

Flank Steak Extraordinaire

1/2 pound flank steak
1/2 cup soy sauce
3-4 tablespoons olive oil (no
  substitutions)

Chives, finely chopped
Coarse ground black pepper

Make small cross-grain cuts on the top length of the flank steak, 1 inch apart. Sprinkle top with chives and black pepper. Add soy sauce. Marinate at least 2 hours in the refrigerator.

Heat a heavy skillet. Add olive oil and beef (uncut side down). Cooking time depends on the thickness of the meat. Sear the outside and keep the inside moist and rare to medium rare. Generally, 10 minutes for the bottom and 5 minutes for the top (sliced side).

When done, remove onto a carving board and slice cross-grain, 1/3-inch thick. Serve on warm plates. Serves 4.

Serve with St. Supéry Cabernet Sauvignon.

Jamie Purviance
St. Supéry Vineyards & Winery

Vietnamese Grilled Beef
Wrapped in Grape Leaves

FIRST GROUP:

1 pound eye of round beef sliced
  1/8 inch thick by 1 inch wide by 2
  inches long
3 tablespoons oyster sauce
1/2 teaspoon curry powder
1 teaspoon sugar or honey
Pepper
2 cloves garlic, finely minced or
  pressed
1 1/2 tablespoons oil

SECOND GROUP:

1 cup finely chopped roasted
  peanuts
Grape leaves, blanched until
  pliable (soak 1/2 hour if
  using jarred variety in several
  changes of water)
1/2 cup very thinly sliced pork
  fat

Marinate the first group of ingredients for 4 to 12 hours. Render very
thin slices of pork fat, 1/2 inch wide and 2 inches long in microwave
until lightly translucent. Lay underside of grape leaf facing you and
place marinated beef strip in middle, topped by pork fat and scatter
with peanuts. Roll up "burrito" style; brush with oil and place on
hinged wire rack and grill. Serve with Nuoc Cham Dipping Sauce and
rice noodles. Serves 6 to 8.

NUOC CHAM DIPPING SAUCE:

4 tablespoons fish sauce
1 tablespoon white rice vinegar
1 tablespoon water
1 1/2 teaspoons sugar

Juice and pulp of one lime
1 clove garlic, minced
Thin slivers of jalapeno, about
  2 medium peppers

Mix and adjust sweet - sour hot balance to your liking.

Serve with Murphy-Goode Cabernet Sauvignon.

Mary Lannin
for
Murphy-Goode Estate Winery

Roasted Pork Tenderloin Stuffed with Spinach, Sundried Tomatoes and Goat Cheese

1 1/2 pounds pork tenderloin, whole
1 bunch spinach, washed, stems removed
3 tablespoons butter
4 cloves garlic, crushed

1/2 cup Champagne
1/4 cup sundried tomatoes
1/4 cup goat cheese
1 tablespoon olive oil
Salt and freshly ground black pepper to taste

Cut a pocket (lengthwise) in the pork.

In a medium saute pan, melt the butter over medium heat. Saute the garlic and spinach. Using a slotted spoon, remove the garlic and spinach and cool. Squeeze out any excess liquid. Chop roughly.

Preheat the oven to 375 degrees. In a small saucepan over medium heat, warm the Champagne. Remove from heat and add the tomatoes. Soak until softened, approximately 15 minutes. Drain the sundried tomatoes and chop roughly. Combine the spinach, sundried tomatoes and crumbled goat cheese. Stuff the pocket with the mixture. Using kitchen string, securely tie the stuffed tenderloin.

In a large saute pan, heat the olive oil. Sear the meat on all sides. Place the seared tenderloin in a shallow roasting pan and roast in the oven for 25 to 30 minutes, or until a meat thermometer, inserted to the center of the tenderloin, registers 140 to 150 degrees. The pork will be slightly pink in the center. This is the suitable doneness for this delicate cut of meat.

Slice the pork into 1/2-inch medallions and fan on serving plates. Serves 4.

Serve with Korbel Champagne Blanc de Noirs.

Teresa Douglas/Mitchell, Culinary Director
Korbel Champagne Cellars

Napa Valley Basil-Smoked Burgers

2 pounds ground sirloin
1/4 cup Zinfandel
1/4 cup lightly packed minced
 fresh basil
1/4 cup minced red onion
1/4 cup fine fresh Italian bread
crumbs
8 sundried tomatoes packed in oil
drained and finely chopped
1 to 2 teaspoons garlic salt
Vegetable oil for brushing on grill
rack
6 large seeded sandwich rolls, split

2/3 cup light mayonnaise
6 slices Monterey jack cheese
2 tablespoons prepared basil
 pesto
Red leaf lettuce leaves
6 large tomato slices, about
 1/4-inch thick
Paper-thin red onion rings
Fresh basil sprigs (optional)
8 fresh basil sprigs moistened
 with water for tossing onto
 the fire

In a grill with a cover, prepare a medium-hot fire for direct-heat cooking. In a medium-sized bowl, lightly combine the sirloin, Zinfandel, minced basil, minced onion, bread crumbs, sundried tomatoes, and garlic salt to taste. Divide the meat mixture into 6 equal portions and shape into round patties. Brush the grill with vegetable oil. Toss the basil sprigs directly onto the coals, then place the patties on the grill and cook, turning once, until done to your preference (5 to 8 minutes on each side).

During the last minute or so of cooking, top each patty with a cheese slice. Meanwhile, in a small bowl, combine the mayonnaise and pesto. Spread the mixture on the cut sides of the toasted rolls. On the bottom half of each roll, layer the lettuce, burger, tomato slice, and onion ring. Add basil sprigs, if desired, and roll tops. Serves 6.

You'll enjoy Sutter Home Zinfandel with these burgers.

Sutter Home Winery

This recipe was the Grand Prize Winner in a national competition by Sutter Home. It won $10,000. It deserved it ... a great recipe, and well worth the effort!

Beef Tenderloin with Porcini, Madeira Cream Sauce

12 slices of beef tenderloin, approximately 1/4-3/8 inch thick
1 ounce dried porcini mushrooms
6 ounces fresh white mushrooms, sliced
2 tablespoons unsalted butter
1 tablespoon extra virgin olive oil
2 cloves garlic, finely minced
1 tablespoon shallot, minced
1/2 cup good quality Madeira

1/2 cup chicken stock (or combination chicken stock and soaking liquid from porcini mushrooms)
1 cup whipping cream
Salt and freshly ground pepper
Minced fresh chervil or Italian parsley, for garnish

Soak dried porcini mushrooms in hot water until softened. Reserve soaking liquid. Rinse, drain and pat dry mushrooms, cut into large pieces.

In a large skillet, heat 1 tablespoon butter and 1 tablespoon of olive oil. When bubbling, add beef and saute about 2 to 3 minutes on each side (or to desired doneness). Remove beef slices and season with salt and pepper. Keep warm.

In the same pan, saute garlic, shallots, fresh mushrooms and porcinis, adding additional butter if needed. Saute for 3 to 4 minutes. Add the Madeira and reduce by one-half.

Add the stock (or combination stock and soaking liquid) and cream. Bring to boil and reduce over moderate heat until slightly thickened. Return beef to pan just to heat through.

Arrange 3 slices per person on warmed dinner plates, nap with sauce and garnish with minced chervil or parsley. Serves 4.

The big, rich taste of the 1990 Perry Creek Cabernet Franc would be a wonderful asset to this flavorful dish.

Alice Chazen, Owner
Perry Creek Vineyards

Jack London Cabernet Peppercorn Sauce

1/4 cup mixed whole peppercorns
(a combination of black, white,
green, pink and red)
1/4 cup Cabernet Sauvignon

1 tablespoon sweet-hot
mustard
1 tablespoon balsamic vinegar
1/2 cup extra virgin olive oil

Grind 1/4 cup peppercorns in spice grinder, or use a mortar and pestle.

Bring 1/4 cup Cabernet Sauvignon to a slight boil. Lower heat and simmer until wine is reduced to 1 tablespoon.

Blend peppercorns, mustard, vinegar and reduced Cabernet in a food processor. Add olive oil very slowly while processor is on. Continue blending after adding oil until sauce is thickened, about 1 to 2 minutes. Refrigerate until ready to use. Sauce will separate if it gets too warm. Makes about 1/2 cup.

You can use this recipe as a marinade and as a basting sauce for grilled meats, chicken or vegetables.

A nice overnight marinade can be made with equal parts of red wine and olive oil along with lots of sliced onions and fresh or dry parsley, sage, thyme and a little rosemary. Be sure to dry your meat well after removing it from the marinade. Barbecue using the Jack London Cabernet Peppercorn Sauce as a basting sauce.

Serve with Kenwood Jack London Cabernet Sauvignon.

A recipe from the Kenwood Collection
Kenwood Vineyards

Grilled Leg of Lamb and Mediterranean Vegetables with Romesco Sauce

One 5- to 6-pound leg of lamb, boned and butterflied (3 to 3 1/2 pounds of meat).

FOR THE LAMB MARINADE:

2 cups full-bodied dry red wine
1/2 cup sherry vinegar or red wine vinegar
1/4 cup olive oil
3 large garlic cloves, minced
1 medium onion, sliced
2 tablespoons chopped fresh rosemary leaves
1 tablespoon chopped fresh thyme, oregano or marjoram leaves
2 teaspoons salt
1 teaspoon freshly ground black pepper

FOR THE ESCALIVADA:

About 2 tablespoons olive oil
2 pounds young, small eggplants (preferably the narrow Japanese variety) cut in half lengthwise
4 large red bell peppers, cut in quarters lengthwise, cored and seeded
1/4 teaspoon salt or to taste
1/4 teaspoon freshly ground black pepper, or to taste
1 tablespoon chopped fresh parsley leaves

Romesco Sauce (recipe follows)

TO PREPARE THE MARINADE:

In a large non-reactive bowl, mix all ingredients for marinade and toss lamb in it. Cover and refrigerate for 3 days, turning lamb at least once each day.

TO COOK THE LAMB AND THE ESCALIVADA:

Light a charcoal fire in a grill with a cover. Rub vegetable skins with about 1 tablespoon oil. Drain lamb and place on grill over red-hot coals. Place vegetables skin-side down around lamb. Grill lamb and vegetables for 25 to 30 minutes. Remove from grill to a plate and let rest for 10 minutes before serving.

While meat rests, peel eggplant and peppers. With your fingers, tear them into very thin strips and arrange on a serving platter. Season vegetables with salt and pepper, drizzle about 1 tablespoon oil over and sprinkle with parsley. Serve with Romesco Sauce. Serves 8.

ROMESCO SAUCE FOR GRILLED MEATS AND VEGETABLES:

1 tablespoon olive oil for frying
1 large (1/2 inch) slice of white bread
1/2 cup whole almonds, toasted for 15 minutes in a preheated 350 degree oven
1/4 teaspoon hot red pepper flakes
1 large clove garlic, coarsely chopped (or 1 teaspoon)
4 medium red bell peppers (about 12 ounces total approx) cored, seeded and cut up (or substitute 4 ounces whole roasted red bell peppers or pimentos from a jar, preferably the fire-roasted ones from Spain)

1/2 pound ripe tomatoes
1/4 teaspoon Spanish paprika
1/4 teaspoon salt or to taste
1/2 teaspoon freshly ground black pepper or to taste
1/4 cup red wine vinegar
1/2 cup extra-virgin olive oil

Heat the 1 tablespoon oil in a small skillet and, over medium heat, fry bread slice until golden on both sides.

Grind toasted almonds finely in the food processor, together with the bread, pepper flakes and garlic. Add red peppers, tomatoes, paprika, salt and pepper and puree until they form a smooth paste. Whirl in vinegar. With the motor running, add oil slowly, in a thin stream. Taste for seasoning. Allow to rest 4 to 5 hours before serving. Yields about 2 1/2 cups.

Salbitxada (pronounced Sahl-bee-tcha-dah) is typically served with "ceballots" (charcoal-grilled Catalan-style leeks). This version of "Romesco" boasts a lively terracotta color and rich harmonious flavors. It is great with other grilled vegetables, too, such as "escalivada" (charcoal-grilled Mediterranean vegetables) and with grilled meats and poultry, especially grilled leg of lamb and grilled chicken.

Wine Recommendation: Serve with a full-bodied red wine, such as Torres Gran Coronas.

Marimar Torres, President
Torres Wines North America
and
The Torres Vineyard and Winery

Roasted Pork Medallion, Lightly Smoked
with a Spicy Thai Sauce

1 1/2 pound pork loin, cut into four
  6-ounce medallions
Salt
Freshly ground pepper

1 tablespoon peanut oil
1/2 cup Port
1 cup veal stock

THAI PASTE:

4 ounces (3/4 cup) unsalted raw
cashews
1 ounce fresh ginger, peeled
1/2 cup plum wine
1/4 cup peanut oil
1/2 cup (3 large) sliced green
onions
1/2 cup chopped cilantro leaves
6 garlic cloves

1 chili pepper, jalapeno or red
  serrano, cored, seeded and
  coarsely chopped
1 1/2 tablespoons turmeric
1 tablespoon honey
1 tablespoon sesame oil
1 tablespoon balsamic vinegar
1 tablespoon cumin
1 teaspoon freshly ground
  white pepper
1/2 teaspoon course salt

To prepare the Thai Paste, preheat oven to 400 degrees. Spread the cashews on a baking tray and roast until golden brown, turning as needed, about 10 minutes. Cool.

In a small pan, cook the ginger in the plum wine until the wine evaporates. With a mortar and pestle, or in a blender, puree all the Thai Paste ingredients. Reserve.

Raise oven temperature to 450 degrees. Season the pork medallions with salt and pepper and flatten slightly with a cleaver or a heavy plate. In an oven-proof skillet, heat the peanut oil. Over high heat, brown both sides of the medallions. Transfer to the oven and roast until medium rare, about 15 minutes. Remove the medallions to a plate and keep warm.

Pour grease from the skillet and deglaze the pan with Port. Pour in the stock and cook over high heat until the sauce thickens slightly. Whisk in 1/4 cup Thai Paste and season to taste with salt, pepper and lime juice. Keep warm. Serves 4.

PRESENTATION:

Cut each medallion into slices. Nap the center of the four warmed plates with sauce and arrange the slices of pork around the sauce.

Suggested wine: Scharffenberger NV Brut Rosé.

Kazuto Matsusaka
for
Scharffenberger Cellars

Kazuto Matsusaka has been the Executive Chef at Wolfgang Puck's Restaurant "Chinois on Main" in Santa Monica for more than 5 years.

Spiced Cherry Cream Sauce

Serve with unseasoned beef, grilled, sauteed or broiled.

4 ounces (1 stick) butter
1/3 cup shallots, finely minced
1-1/2 cups beef stock (unsalted or low-salt, preferably homemade)
2/3 cup heavy cream
1-1/2 cups canned tart red cherries, finely chopped

1/4 cup juice from cherries
1/4 cup black pepper, finely ground
1 1/2 tablespoons Dijon-style mustard
1 1/2 tablespoons lemon juice
1 1/2 teaspoons powdered cinnamon

In butter, saute shallots over medium heat, stirring frequently until soft and translucent. Add beef stock and continue cooking, stirring occasionally, until liquid is reduced by half. Add cream; continue cooking and stirring until liquid is again reduced by half. Add remaining ingredients and continue cooking, stirring occasionally, until sauce is thick and creamy. Makes 2 cups, serves 8.

This recipe was developed for Kendall-Jackson Vintner's Reserve Pinot Noir. A medium-bodied wine with good acidity, it has aromas of cherry and cranberry with black pepper spice and smooth vanilla from oak aging. This sauce ties in with the cherries and slight black pepper in the wine. The cream contrasts nicely with the wine's crisp acidity; the spicy mustard contrasts with and brings out the fruit.

Kendall-Jackson Vineyards

Blue Cheese Tenderloin with Merlot Sauce

3 pounds pork tenderloin
6 ounces fresh blue cheese
3/4 cup whipping cream
1/2 cup butter
1 tablespoon flour

1/2 cup Merlot wine
1/2 tablespoon fresh ground
 black pepper
1/2 pint fresh raspberries

Pat entire tenderloin(s) with black pepper. Melt 1/4 cup butter and Merlot together in a hot, non-stick pan and braise seasoned tenderloin. Place tenderloin aside in an oblong glaco baking pan. Add remaining butter, sprinkles of flour and whipping cream to the seasoned pan, using a whisk to blend until smooth and creamy. Pour mixture over tenderloin and crumble blue cheese over the top of the roast. Bake on 350 degrees for 45 minutes. Serve with fresh summer squash and sundried tomatoes. Garnish with raspberries. Serves 6.

Serve with Beaucanon Merlot.

Deborah Thorman, Hospitality Director
Beaucanon Winery

Beef Saute with Olives

1-1 1/2 pounds lean quality beef
stew meat
1 large onion, sliced
1/2 large red pepper, sliced
4-ounce jar red pimento, minced
20-24 stuffed green olives, sliced
Salt and pepper to taste
1 teaspoon fines herbes

Flour
1 cup sweet vermouth
2-3 sprigs of fresh parsley,
chopped
1 can stewed or sliced
tomatoes (14 1/2 ounces)
2 tablespoons oil

Cut meat in small pieces (approximately 1 inch). Season with fines herbes. Shake a light dusting of flour over meat. Brown in large skillet or casserole a small amount at a time. Add sliced onions, sliced red pepper, and continue cooking, stirring and turning until onions begin to cook. Add minced olives and pimento, stir, and add 1 cup vermouth. Bring to a simmer, then turn heat down to low.

Let simmer for 1/2 hour. Then add tomatoes. Continue to simmer. If liquid gets low, add more vermouth as needed. Sprinkle chopped parsley on meat and continue to cook until meat is tender. If sauce needs thickening, add small amount of flour.

Serve with rice or noodles. Serves 4.

With this dish, you will particularly enjoy Conn Creek 1988 Napa Valley Cabernet Sauvignon.

Conn Creek Winery

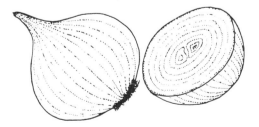

Mother's Lamb Stew

2 pounds lamb stew meat,
 carefully trimmed
2-3 tablespoons olive oil
1/2 cup diced onions
1/2 cup diced carrots
2 garlic cloves, minced
1 wedge unpeeled orange

1 large strip lemon peel
1 cup Zinfandel
1 cup tomato juice
6 whole cloves
1 stick cinnamon
1 teaspoon powdered
 coriander

In a medium-sized Dutch oven, brown lamb lightly in hot olive oil. Add onions, carrots and garlic and saute briefly. Add rest of ingredients. Cover and bring to a simmer on top of the stove. Place in a preheated 325 degree oven and bake until tender, about 1-1/2 to 2 hours. Check occasionally. If more liquid is needed, add equal parts Zinfandel and tomato juice. De-grease and thicken sauce with flour and water if necessary.

Serve with brown rice and a green salad. This dish goes well with our Ravenswood Vintners Blend Zinfandel.

Joel Peterson, Winemaker
Ravenswood Winery

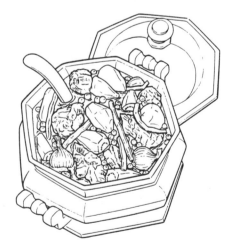

SEAFOOD

Mahi Mahi with Avocado and Tobiko Salsa

4 pieces fresh Mahi Mahi (3-4 ounces each) or other firm-fleshed fish
1/3 cup soy sauce
1/4 cup fresh lime juice

1 teaspoon freshly chopped garlic
1 1/2 teaspoon freshly grated ginger

Place Mahi Mahi and next four ingredients in glass dish and let marinate 2 to 3 hours in refrigerator, turning fish occasionally. Wipe off fish and lightly dust each piece with flour and shake off excess. Brush lightly with oil and put on hot grill or preheated pan. Cook 3 to 4 minutes on each side and serve with Avocado and Tobiko Salsa.

AVOCADO AND TOBIKO SALSA:

1 Haas avocado, peeled and cut in 1/2-inch dice
2-3 tablespoons Tobiko (Flying Fish eggs)*
1/4 teaspoon chopped fresh garlic

1 tablespoon chopped cilantro
1-2 teaspoons lime juice
Splash of safflower oil
2-3 scallions, finely chopped
Salt and pepper

* Small grain caviar may be substituted.

Mix all ingredients (except avocado) well and season to your liking. Add avocado and toss gently.

So tasty with our Matanzas Creek Chardonnay.

Sarah Kaswan, Chef
Matanzas Creek Winery

Spiced Poached Salmon

2 quarts water	3 carrots, sliced
1 bottle dry white wine	1 bay leaf
2 medium onions, stuck with 2	1/2 teaspoon thyme
whole cloves each	1/2 teaspoon salt
2 stalks celery, sliced	3-4 pound salmon, whole

PICKLING LIQUID:

1 quart rice vinegar
1/2 cup pickling spices
1/2 cup sugar

In a fish poacher or pan that will comfortably hold the fish, place the 2 quarts water, wine, onions, celery, carrots, bay leaf, thyme, and salt, and simmer for 1 hour to make a bouillon. Add the fish on a poaching rack or wrapped in a double thickness of cheesecloth, leaving long ends of cloth for easy removal of fish. (Measure the fish at its thickest point, then poach for 10 minutes per inch.) When fish is cooked, remove from stock and set aside to cool. Carefully remove the skin from the salmon and place fish in a deep dish. Pour over pickling liquid and chill for 24 to 48 hours. Drain and serve garnished with watercress.

Wine Suggestion: Dry Chenin Blanc

Katie Wetzel Murphy
Alexander Valley Vineyards

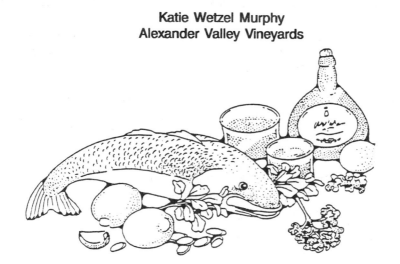

All Seasons Cafe Bamboo Skewered Salmon with Oriental Greens and Soy Dressing

8 3-ounce strips of salmon
2 1-inch pieces of fresh ginger
2 ounces Indonesian Ketjap
 (available in specialty shops)
2 ounces sesame oil

4 cloves garlic, finely chopped
8 8-inch bamboo skewers
2 bunches of Mitzuna or other
 Oriental greens such as red
 mustard

Salmon filets can be cut by your local fish monger into approximately 3-ounce strips. Place salmon into a glass or stainless steel pan. Smash the 2 pieces of ginger with a heavy cleaver to release some of the juices inside the ginger. Using your hands, squeeze the ginger juice onto the salmon pieces. Sprinkle the garlic over the salmon. Mix the sesame oil and Indonesian Ketjap together in a bowl and pour over the salmon strips. Marinate for at least 15 minutes to 24 hours. Gently push the salmon strips onto the bamboo skewers leaving a small handle on each end.

DRESSING:

2 ounces soy sauce
2 ounces sesame oil
2 ounces fresh orange juice

2 sweet oranges
2 tablespoons sesame seeds

To cook the salmon, place the bamboo-skewered salmon strips onto a preheated grill and cook 4 to 5 minutes on each side or until done.

To prepare dressing, place orange juice, soy sauce and sesame oil into a bowl and whisk together. Peel and section the two oranges. Add the orange sections into the dressing mixture.

To complete the salad, toss the greens with the dressing and divide equally between four plates. Place the salmon strips on top of the greens and sprinkle with sesame seeds. Serve immediately. Serves 4.

Mark Dierkhising, Chef & Owner
All Seasons Cafe

Curried Lobster and Mushroom Tartlets

2 tablespoons sweet butter
1/4 cup finely chopped onion
1 1/2 teaspoons curry powder
1/4 pound chantrelle or hedgehog
  mushrooms, or 6 ounces standard
  commercial mushrooms

1/2 cup heavy cream
1 teaspoon cornstarch
1 tablespoon chardonnay
1 cup chopped cooked lobster
  (about 6 ounces)*

In a heavy saucepan, heat the butter and saute the onion without browning over medium-low heat until translucent. Add the curry powder and saute for a few seconds to release the flavors. Add the cream. Dissolve cornstarch in wine and stir into cream. Bring to a boil, stirring frequently, then simmer slowly until the sauce is very thick.

Clean and chop the mushrooms. In a large skillet, heat the remaining tablespoon of butter and when very hot, add the mushrooms. Saute until mushrooms are lightly browned and tender. Add to the curry sauce along with salt. Simmer a minute or two, then add lobster. Taste and add more salt if required.

If you're ready to fill the tartlet shells, cook just until lobster is heated through. Otherwise remove from heat and set aside until needed. Can be refrigerated for two days. Reheat quickly, stirring frequently as overcooking will destroy the lobster's delicate flavor and texture. Fill the tartlet shells and serve.

*If you don't want to deal with a whole lobster, buy a lobster tail and steam it. Cooked crab would also work well in this recipe.

PASTRY:**

6 ounces sweet butter, chilled
1 1/2 cups all purpose flour

1/4 teaspoon salt
3-4 tablespoons Chardonnay,
  cold

Cut the chilled butter into pieces and combine with flour and salt in a bowl or food processor. Process until mixture is mealy. Add 3 tablespoons wine and pulse a few times. Transfer to a bowl and finish blending by hand, adding more wine only if necessary to hold dough together. Form dough into a ball, wrap in plastic wrap and refrigerate for at least 1/2 hour to relax gluten before rolling.

Dough can be made up to 3 days in advance and refrigerated. Roll out dough quite thin on a lightly floured board. Cut into circles and fit into small tartlet tins or miniature muffin pans, pressing in well. Prick with fork. Gather up remaining dough and roll out again.

Refrigerate at least 20 minutes before baking. Bake in a preheated 425 degree oven for about 15 minutes or until nicely browned. After 5 minutes, if pastry seems to be puffing too much, push down gently with back of a teaspoon, otherwise you may not have a shell to fit. The tartlets are best when baked no more than an hour or two in advance.

** If you prefer something simpler to prepare, use one of these alternatives to making the pastry tarts.

TOAST CASES:

24 slices commercial "thin-sliced"   2 tablespoons butter
 bread

Cut bread into rounds with a cutter. Melt butter and brush bread rounds generously. Brush small tartlet tins or miniature muffin pans with butter. Press bread rounds into pans firmly. Bake in a 425 degree oven for about 6 minutes or until nicely browned. Remove toast cases from pans and cool on a rack. The cases will crisp as they cool. Should any seem moist, return to the hot oven for a minute. Can be made an hour or two in advance.

MELBA TOASTS:

24 slices commercial "thin-sliced"   2 tablespoons butter
 bread

Stack bread slices and trim off crusts. Cut slices in half on the diagonal to make 24 triangles. Melt butter and brush triangles generously. Brush a baking sheet with butter and place triangles on it. Bake in a 425 degree oven until golden brown, about 5 minutes. Remove from oven. When cool, the toasts should be crisp and dry. If moist, return to oven for another minute. The toasts can be made several hours in advance.

Wine: 1987 Sterling Vineyards Diamond Mountain Chardonnay.

**Richard Alexei, Food & Wine Consultant
Sterling Vineyards**

Abalone Crab Chowder

1 1/2 cups abalone scraps (or clams)
1 cup fresh crab meat
1 1/2 cup potatoes, diced
4 pieces smoked bacon
2 onions
2 cups half & half (or whole milk)
1 lemon
4 tablespoons fresh chives, minced
White pepper, cayenne pepper
4-6 cloves

4-6 fresh mushrooms
1 bay leaf, broken
1 cube butter (8 tablespoons)
8 tablespoons flour
4 cups chicken stock, hot
1 tablespoon butter
1/2 teaspoon garlic powder
1/4 teaspoon liquid smoke flavoring
Creamed horseradish

To prepare abalone, separate from "guts" and remove from shell. Trim rough outer edge (with black discoloration) from perimeter of abalone. Scrub this with a brush or plastic "chore girl" and water to remove black. Chop in food processor using ON/OFF. Transfer to colander and rinse well with running water. Pick fresh crab from shell. Keep shellfish separate but toss each with fresh lemon and garlic powder. Refrigerate until needed.

Brush to clean fresh mushrooms; slice and reserve. Peel and chop one onion, stud the other with 4 to 6 cloves. Peel and dice potatoes; cover with water to keep from browning. Place studded onion and broken bay leaf in half and half and bring to a boil. Turn off heat and let steep in liquid. Reserve.

In a heavy pot, melt 1 cube of butter. Add flour and continue to stir over low heat for approximately five minutes to break down flour glutens. Add hot chicken stock to cooked roux, using a whisk. Stir until blended, then simmer over medium-low heat for 15 minutes.

While stock is simmering, cook bacon in a heavy saute pan. Pat dry and chop; reserve for garnish. Drain bacon grease from pan, then add one tablespoon butter and saute chopped onion until translucent and add to cooking stock. Add abalone. Drain diced potatoes and add to chowder and continue to cook for about 15 minutes, stirring occasionally. Pour half and half through sieve and add to chowder, stirring occasionally and cook for another 15 minutes.

Five minutes before serving, add crab, fresh mushrooms and adjust seasoning to taste with salt, liquid smoke flavoring, touch of white and cayenne pepper or horseradish. Ladle into hot soup bowls and garnish with chopped bacon and fresh chives. Serves 6.

Serve with McDowell Fumé Blanc.

Richard Keehn, Proprietor
McDowell Valley Vineyard

Other delicious ingredients for a variation of flavor are sundried tomatoes, roasted red or yellow peppers or smoked tomato creme frâiche. If creme frâiche is not available, mix a seasoning into sour cream.

Grilled Salmon with Orange-Saffron Butter

6 salmon steaks (1-inch thick)
Vegetable oil
Salt and pepper to taste

Heat grill. Brush fish with oil and season with salt and pepper. Grill on each side for 4 to 5 minutes.

SAUCE:

5 tablespoons butter	1 tablespoon orange zest
1/4 teaspoon saffron	2 teaspoons chopped shallots
1 tablespoon orange juice	Salt and pepper to taste

Dissolve saffron in the orange juice. Place all ingredients into a food processor or blender and puree. Sauce may be prepared in advance and stored in the refrigerator for up to a week. Serve salmon with a dollop of saffron butter, julienned summer vegetables and Franciscan Oakville Estate Chardonnay. Serves 6.

Franciscan Vineyards, Inc.

Tuna with Lavender

3 pounds fresh tuna, cut in 1-inch slices
2 tablespoons whole black peppercorns
2 tablespoons Szechuan peppercorns
2 tablespoons fresh or 4 tablespoons dried lavender flowers and/or buds*

2 tablespoons olive oil
2 tablespoons butter
3 tablespoons minced shallots
1 cup chicken stock
1 cup Cabernet Sauvignon
4 tablespoons softened butter

Crush peppercorns with pestle, or process with steel blade in food processor. Mix pepper with lavender and press into both sides of the tuna slices. Cover and let stand at least 1/2 hour, up to 3 hours for maximum pepper flavor. Sear over high heat in butter and oil 3 to 4 minutes on each side. (This is a dish that can be served rare. Check for desired doneness by piercing with the point of a small, sharp knife.)

Hold fish in a warm oven while making the sauce. Add shallots to saute pan and cook about 1 minute. Deglaze the pan with the stock, then add the Cabernet and cook rapidly until reduced by half. Remove pan from heat and stir in butter. Pour sauce over tuna and serve immediately. Serves 6.

*Dried lavender is available in many health food stores.

Suggested wine: Simi Cabernet Sauvignon.

Mary Evely, Chef
Simi Winery

Citrus and Apricot Prawns

INGREDIENTS STEP 1:

12 large prawns
2-3 tablespoons olive oil
1 tablespoon fresh ginger, finely
 chopped
1/2 cup fresh scallions, chopped
2 tablespoons fresh parsley, finely
 chopped
1 tablespoon white wine
1 tablespoon fresh chives,
chopped

Juice of 1/2 orange
Juice of 1/2 lime
Juice of 1 lemon
3 tablespoons Grand Marnier
 Liqueur
2 tablespoons candied ginger,
 finely chopped
Zest the rind of 1/2 lemon, 1/2
 orange and 1/2 lime

INGREDIENTS STEP 2:

1/2 cup dried apricots, cut into thin
 strips
1 cup papaya, diced

2 tablespoons fresh scallions,
 chopped
2 tablespoons fresh parsley,
 chopped

Wash the prawns, removing the shell but leaving the tail on, and deveining. Place on a plate and pat dry with a paper towel. In a saucepan, heat the olive oil and add the fresh ginger, scallions, and parsley. Saute until the scallions are soft and then add the prawns, wine and chives and continue to stir. As the prawns begin to turn pink in color, add the lemon, lime and orange juice along with the Grand Marnier and candied ginger. Let simmer for a minute or two while adding the three citrus rinds.

At the last moment, add the dried apricots and papaya and toss to mix. Sprinkle some fresh scallions and parsley for color. Serves 4.

Serve with Heitz Cellar Grignolino Rosé.

This recipe evolved from my fondness of prawns and tropical fruits. I like it best served warm, though it can also be served cold with the addition of ingredients from Step 2 right before serving so that the fruit will not become mushy. If you cannot find fresh papaya, mango or nectarines also work well or any combination thereof.

Kathleen Heitz
Heitz Wine Cellars

Foxy Loxburgers

1 1/2 pounds fresh salmon, boned, skinned and ground
1 teaspoon freshly squeezed lemon juice
1 tablespoon minced onion
1 tablespoon minced fresh dill or 1 teaspoon dried dill
1 tablespoon dry sherry

Vegetable oil for brushing on grill rack
4 bagels, split
3 ounces cream cheese, softened
1 tablespoon butter, melted
8 thin slices sweet onion such as Maui or Walla Walla
Fresh dill sprigs (optional)

In a grill with a cover, prepare a medium-hot fire for direct-heat cooking.

In a medium-sized bowl, combine the salmon, lemon juice, minced onion, minced dill and dry sherry. Mix well. Divide the mixture into 8 equal portions and shape into round patties.

Brush the grill rack with vegetable oil. Place the patties on the grill rack and cook, turning once, until done to your preference (4 to 6 minutes on each side). During the last few minutes of cooking, place the bagels, cut side down, on the outer edges of the grill to toast lightly.

Meanwhile, in a small bowl, combine the cream cheese and butter and blend thoroughly.

Spread the cream cheese mixture on the cut side of each warm bagel half, then top each half with an onion slice and a salmon patty. Top with dill sprigs, if desired. Serves 8.

Serve with Sutter Home Zinfandel.

Sutter Home Winery

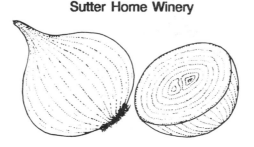

Beaucanon Scampi Dijonnaise with Garlic Tomato Pasta

3 tablespoons olive oil
24 cleaned jumbo shrimp
11 cloves minced garlic
2 minced shallots
1/2 cup fresh basil
1/4 cup lemon juice

2 tablespoons Dijon mustard
1/2 cup Cabernet Sauvignon
1 tablespoon sweet unsalted
  butter
Salt and pepper to taste

Add olive oil to heated skillet. Mix garlic and shallots together, then saute half the mixture for 1 minute. Then, add shrimp and shake and cook on one side shaking the mixture so it won't stick or burn. Turn shrimp, add remaining garlic/shallot mixture and cook for 1 minute. Pour in Cabernet Sauvignon and continue cooking for 2 minutes. Set aside sauteed shrimp. Add lemon, Dijon mustard and basil to the sauce from the shrimp and simmer until thickened. Add butter, salt and pepper to taste. Toss in shrimp and serve on tomato pasta.

GARLIC TOMATO PASTA:

8 ounces linguini
3 tablespoons olive oil
2 cloves minced garlic

3 medium tomatoes, cleaned
  and quartered
1/2 cup fresh parsley

Cook pasta to package directions. Heat oil in a saute pan and saute garlic for 1 to 2 minutes. Add tomatoes and continue cooking for 1 to 2 minutes. Add parsley and toss with linguini. Present by making a bed of linguini, then top with shrimp and sauce. Serves 4 to 6.

Serve with Beaucanon Cabernet Sauvignon.

Deborah Thorman, Hospitality Director
Beaucanon Winery

Broiled Seafood Brochettes
with Tandoori Sauce

4 scallions, trimmed and minced
2 cloves garlic, minced
4 tablespoons fresh cilantro,
 minced
1 tablespoon lime zest, grated
1 tablespoon fresh ginger, minced
1/4 teaspoon fresh ground pepper
1/8 teaspoon ground cumin
1/8 teaspoon red pepper flakes

3 tablespoons olive oil
3 tablespoons lime juice
1/4 cup Fumé Blanc
1/2 cup plain low fat yogurt
16 prawns, peeled and
 de-veined
12 sea scallops or cubes of
swordfish or lobster
 medallions
Skewers

Combine all ingredients except prawns and scallops in a mixing bowl. Blend thoroughly and set aside. Start broiler. Skewer fish, starting with a prawn, then a scallop. Continue the process, ending with four prawns and three scallops per skewer. Broil 2 to 3 minutes per side. Remove from broiler. Spoon the Tandoori sauce over the skewers; return to broiler. Cook 2 more minutes. Serves 4.

Excellent with Dry Creek Vineyard Fumé Blanc.

Brad Wallace
for
Dry Creek Vineyard

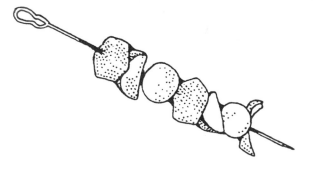

Shrimp and Vegetable Pasta

2 pounds large shrimp, de-veined and peeled
2 yellow bell peppers, seeded, cored and cut into 1/4-inch pieces
2 red bell peppers, seeded, cored and cut into 1/4-inch pieces
7 ripe plum tomatoes, cut into 1/2-inch pieces
1/2 cup chopped fresh dill
2 tablespoons dried tarragon
2 tablespoons chopped shallots
1/4 teaspoon dried red pepper flakes
1 teaspoon ground black pepper
1 teaspoon salt
1/2 cup fresh lemon juice
1 cup olive oil
1/4 teaspoon hot chile oil
1 head broccoli, cut into small florets
2 cups cooked peas
1 pound linguine

Two hours ahead, bring large pot of water to a boil. Drop in shrimp and cook until tender, about 1 minute. Drain and rinse under cool water and place in large bowl. Add tomatoes, bell peppers, dill, tarragon, red pepper flakes, shallots, black pepper, lemon juice, salt, olive oil, and chili oil to the bowl of shrimp. Toss well, cover and refrigerate.

Bring a large saucepan of water to a boil, drop in broccoli florets and cook for about 1 minute. Drain. Mix the peas and broccoli with shrimp and vegetables. Cook the pasta, drain it, and toss it with the shrimp and vegetable sauce. Serve immediately.

Wine suggestion: Alexander Valley Vineyard Dry Chenin Blanc or Chardonnay

Katie Wetzel Murphy
Alexander Valley Vineyards

Sole Fillets in Herb Cream

4 sole fillets, each about 6 ounces
Salt and freshly ground premium
 quality white pepper
4 teaspoons minced fresh tarragon
 leaves
2 teaspoons finely chopped fresh
 basil leaves

1 teaspoon minced fresh
 thyme leaves
3 tablespoons unsalted butter
1/2 cup heavy (whipping)
 cream

(You can use dry instead of fresh herbs: about 1 teaspoon crumbled dry tarragon and 1 scant teaspoon crumbled dry basil. No thyme.)

Wipe fish dry. Arrange in a single layer in a large buttered frying or fish-poaching pan. Season with salt and pepper; sprinkle with tarragon, basil and thyme; dot with butter. Bake in a 400 degree oven until fish becomes opaque almost to center and barely separates when tested with a spoon, about 5 to 6 minutes. Baste once or twice. Lift fish to serving plates. Add cream to juices in pan. Cook and stir over direct heat just to blend and reduce slightly to a sauce the consistency of heavy cream. Season with salt and pepper. Spoon over fish. Makes 4 servings.

Garnish with a fresh sprig of one of the herbs.

You can bake fish in a dish which will not take direct heat: Remove baked fillets to serving plates, transfer baking juices to a small pan and make a slender sauce as directed.

Cook fish slightly less done than you want at serving, since fish continues to cook a little once out of the pan. Needed cooking time will vary, depending upon fish and its thickness.

Add a colorful and luscious embellishment if you can. Turn small pieces of beautifully steamed Maine lobster or fresh crab in melted butter to cloak well and to barely heat; season with salt and white pepper. Spoon in an arc alongside fish.

Serve with Roederer Estate Anderson Valley Brut.

Roederer Estate

Southern Seafood Stew

1/2 pound bacon, diced
2 carrots, finely diced
3 onions, thinly sliced
4 cloves garlic, crushed or minced
3 cups fresh or canned plum
 tomatoes
1 pound red potatoes, halved
1 cup clam juice
1/2 cup Rouge Champagne
1/2 teaspoon dried thyme
Pinch of sugar
2 cups chicken stock

Salt and pepper to taste
1/2 pound smoked sausages,
 sliced
2 dozen clams (whole or
 canned)
1 pound medium shrimp,
 peeled
1/2 pound white fish, small
 chunks
1/4 teaspoon cayenne pepper
 (optional)

Saute the bacon with the carrots, onions and garlic. Drain half the grease. Add the tomatoes, potatoes, clam juice and Champagne. Sprinkle in the thyme and sugar, simmer for 30 minutes. Add the stock and correct the seasonings. Bring the stew to a low boil. Add the fish; simmering briefly until the flesh is just cooked.

Serve hot with crusty French bread. Serves 8. Serve with Korbel Rouge Champagne.

Teresa Douglas/Mitchell, Culinary Director
Korbel Champagne Cellars

Teresa Douglas/Mitchell, Culinary Director for Korbel, graduated from the California Culinary Academy with honors, after a career in television and film production. She apprenticed with Bradley Ogden, then was the Chef at the Vintner's Inn, and then to John Ash & Company, prior to joining Korbel.

She is responsible for developing menus to accompany Korbel Champagnes.

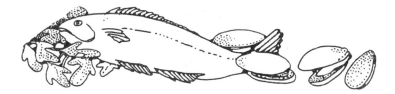

Sole a la Gewurztraminer

7 tablespoons butter
2 tablespoons chopped parsley
2 pound sole
1/3 cup dry bread crumbs

1 cup Gewurztraminer wine
Salt and pepper
4 tablespoons heavy cream

Dot a large, shallow dish with 1/2 the butter and sprinkle with 1/2 parsley. Place sole in dish. Sprinkle rest of parsley and bread crumbs and dot with rest of butter. Pour in the Gewurztraminer; season with salt and pepper. Place in a 350 degree oven and let fish simmer (not boil) for 15 to 20 minutes or until fish is cooked. Just before serving, add cream. Serve from dish. Serves 4.

Serve with Crunchy Cabbage Slaw (recipe follows).

Carolann Heyden
Mark West Winery

Crunchy Cabbage Slaw

1/2 cup mayonnaise
1 tablespoon red wine vinegar
1 tablespoon Gewurztraminer
1/2 teaspoon dijon mustard
1/2 cup toasted pinoles (pine nuts)

1/2 head of medium-sized cabbage
1 green scallion
4 broccoli flowerlets
1/2 medium red pepper

Slice cabbage head into thin slivers. Put into large bowl. Chop scallion, including green tops. Slice red pepper lengthwise into julienne strips and add to cabbage.

For dressing, mix together mayonnaise, vinegar, Gewurztraminer, mustard and pinoles. Toss dressing and slaw ingredients together. Refrigerate until ready to serve. Serves 4 to 6.

Serve with 1989 Mark West Gewurztraminer.

Eunice Marion
Mark West Winery

Scallops in Saffron Chardonnay Sauce

3 tablespoons finely chopped
  shallots
2 tablespoons unsalted butter
1 1/2 cups fish stock
1 cup Chardonnay
1 cup heavy cream

1/4-1/2 teaspoon saffron
  threads, crumbled
Grated rind and juice of 1/2
  orange
Small pinch dried red chili
  pepper flakes
Salt and white pepper to taste

In a heavy saucepan, saute shallots in butter for a few minutes, until translucent. Add fish stock and wine, boil until reduced by half. Add cream and reduce by half again, or until mixture coats back of spoon. Strain. Return to saucepan. Add saffron, orange zest and juice, red chili pepper flakes, and salt and pepper to taste. Keep sauce warm. Makes about 1 cup sauce.

SCALLOPS:

1 1/2 pounds whole fresh sea scallops
4 tablespoons unsalted butter

Saute scallops in melted butter until warmed through and just opaque, only a few minutes. Using a slotted spoon, divide scallops onto warmed serving plates and top with hot sauce. Garnish as desired. Serves 4 as a main course, 6 as a first course.

Serve with Mirassou Chardonnay and sweet French bread.

Mirassou

133

Seared Peppered Tuna
with Chive Potatoes, Red Wine and Orange

6 tuna steaks, 3/4 inch thick, approx 6 ounces each
1 3/4 cups fresh cracked black pepper
1 egg white
6 medium to large russet potatoes
2 ounces heavy cream

3 ounces creme frâiche
3 ounces unsalted butter
2 bunches chives, finely chopped
Zest of 2 oranges, finely julienned, blanched 5 seconds and refreshed in cold water

SAUCE:

1 bottle Cabernet
1 quart veal stock
5 shallots, peeled, rough chopped
5 cloves garlic, rough chopped
15 black peppercorns
1 sprig tarragon

1 sprig thyme
3 tablespoons butter, unsalted, cubed
Sea salt and freshly ground black pepper

In a large pot, combine all ingredients for sauce except butter, and reduce by 2/3; whisk in cold butter, strain through mesh-like sieve. Season with sea salt and fresh pepper.

Peel and cut potatoes in sixths and place in cold water. Cook until the potatoes can be pierced easily with a fork. Drain. Put through a food mill, potato ricer or mesh sieve. Mix in heavy cream, 3 ounces unsalted butter and creme frâiche. Season with sea salt and ground black pepper.

Brush the tuna steaks with egg white and gently press in cracked black pepper on both sides of steaks. Sprinkle with fine sea salt. Heat a large frying pan. Add olive oil, then add tuna steaks. Cook till medium rare over medium high heat.

To serve, place potatoes in the center of the plate and top with tuna. Distribute the orange zest over the tuna and around. Pour the red wine sauce lightly over the tuna and around the plate. Serves 6.

Serve with J. Lohr Estates Seven Oaks Cabernet.

Christopher Majer, Chef
Splendido, San Francisco
for
J. Lohr Winery

Salmon Poached in Champagne and Cream Sauce with Fresh Papaya

2 cups Champagne or sparkling wine
2 cups heavy whipping cream
2 tablespoons unsalted butter

4 6-ounce salmon fillets
1 papaya, peeled, seeded and quartered

Put Champagne in skillet large enough to hold the salmon fillets. Bring to a boil and reduce by half. Add cream and return to boil. Simmer salmon in mixture for 5 minutes. Place papaya quarter, which has been cut into a fan, on top of each fillet and continue to cook until the salmon is done, about 3 more minutes. It should be firm to touch, but still moist in the center. Remove salmon from pan and keep warm. Reduce sauce to about 1 or 1 1/4 cups. Whisk in 2 tablespoons of butter and pour over salmon. Serves 4.

Wine Recommendation: Benziger of Glen Ellen Blanc de Blancs.

Stella Fleming, Executive Chef
Glen Ellen Winery

Broiled Salmon with Cucumbers

2 tablespoons olive oil
1/4 cup shallots, chopped
1/2 cup Chardonnay
1 cup cream or half and half
1 tablespoon lemon juice
4 salmon fillets

2 cucumbers, peeled and
  sliced in thin lengthwise
  sections
1/4 cup fresh dill, chopped
Salt and pepper

Saute the shallots in one tablespoon of the olive oil until golden; then add Chardonnay and bring to a boil. After boiling about a minute, blend in the cream and lemon juice and boil until the sauce is reduced to about 1 cup.

Brush the salmon with the remaining olive oil and broil until just cooked through on each side (3 to 5 minutes per side). While the salmon is broiling, steam the cucumber slices until soft.

Warm the sauce and season with dill, salt and pepper. Drain the cucumbers and place a bed of them on each plate, then place a salmon fillet on each bed of cucumbers. Spoon the warm sauce over each fillet. Serves 4.

Serve with a bottle of Windsor Chardonnay.

Windsor Vineyards

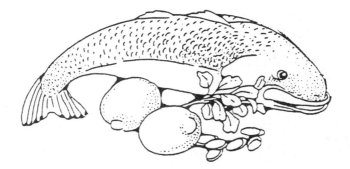

Mediterranean Fish Stew

(A)
1 pound chopped fish (your choice
  of fillet of sole, snapper, scallops,
  crab, or a combination of fish)
1 cup chopped onion
2 cloves crushed garlic
2 cups clamato juice
3 tablespoons lemon juice
1 bay leaf
1/4 teaspoon pepper
1 13-ounce can crushed tomatoes
3/4 cup chopped celery
1/3 cup chopped bell pepper

(B)
3 cups diced cooked red
  potatoes

(C)
2 tablespoons butter
2 tablespoons flour
2 tablespoons chopped fresh
  sweet basil
1 tablespoon chopped parsley
2 bottles dry Chenin Blanc

Simmer (A) minus fish for 1/2 hour. Add (B) and fish and simmer 15
minutes more. Melt butter from (C) in a small pan and stir in flour.
Add rest of (C) to mixture of (A) and (B) along with basil and parsley.
Allow to heat through a minute or two and serve. Serves 6.

Enjoy with our Dry Chenin Blanc.

Laura Spinetta
Charles Spinetta Winery and Gallery

*We queried Laura about the two bottles of wine for this recipe. She
assured us that ". . . we have served this many times to our guests at
our winery. Everyone loves it." We tried it, and she's right. VMH*

Lobster Mousseline

6 ounces scallops, trimmed
8 ounces sole or halibut filets
1 egg
1 egg white
1 tablespoon lemon juice
1/2 teaspoon salt
1/2 teaspoon pepper
2 tablespoons butter

1/3 cup reduced lobster stock (see directions for stock below) Prepared fish stock can be substituted for lobster stock
1 1/2 cups heavy cream
3/4 cup chopped lobster meat (meat from medium lobster, approximately 1 1/2 pounds) See directions for cooking lobster below

All ingredients must be well chilled.

Puree scallops, fish, the egg and egg white in a food processor until smooth. Keep chilled.

In a mixer, beat together the butter, lemon juice, salt and pepper. Bit by bit, add the fish puree and the lobster stock to the butter mixture. In a steady stream, add the cream. Beat for two minutes until uniform. By hand, fold in chopped lobster meat.

Pack mixture into 12 buttered ramequins or one terrine lined with buttered wax paper. Cover with buttered wax paper.

Place in a pan of boiling water that reaches at least halfway up the sides.   Bake in a 350 degree oven until just firm and springy. Individual ramequins will take 8 to 10 minutes, a terrine will take 30 to 40 minutes, depending on size.

Terrine: Chill several hours or overnight before unmolding. Slice into twelve pieces and serve with Sauce Cardinal (see recipe below).

Ramequins: Ramequins can be unmolded immediately and may be served warm or chilled. Serve with Sauce Cardinal (see recipe below). Serves 12.

SAUCE CARDINAL:

2 cups lobster stock
2 cups heavy cream

1/2 cup butter

Combine lobster stock and heavy cream. Over medium heat, reduce to 1 cup. Remove from heat and whisk in reserved roe and lobster liver (tomalley). At the last minute, with mousseline already in place to serve, whisk in butter.

COOKING THE LOBSTER:

Place live lobster in a large pot of rapidly boiling, salted water. Boil for approximately 12 minutes. Cook, crack and pick out lobster meat.

Save shells for stock. Reserve roe and lobster liver (tomalley) for the sauce.

LOBSTER STOCK:

1 onion	2 tomatoes, chopped
1 stalk celery	2 sprigs parsley
1 carrot	2 sprigs tarragon (or 1/2
Shell from one lobster	teaspoon dried)
2 tablespoons butter	3/4 cup white wine

Coarsely chop onion, celery and carrot. "Sweat" them (i.e. saute gently without butter or oil) for 10 minutes in a 1 to 2 gallon stock pot.

Coarsely break up lobster shells. Saute in butter until bright red. Add to vegetables in stock pot. Add chopped tomato, parsley, tarragon and wine. Cover with cold water. Bring to boil, turn heat down and simmer 1 hour.

Optional, but recommended: Allow stock to cool slightly and then grind up the shells and vegetables in a food processor. Return to stock pot and simmer 1 more hour. Stir frequently to prevent scorching.

Strain off stock liquid, being careful to eliminate all bits of shell and sand. To do this, strain first through a sieve and then again through cheesecloth. Return strained stock to the pot and boil slowly, reducing it down to 2 to 3 cups.

Serve with Piper Sonoma 1982 Brut Reserve.

Michael Hirschberg and Shiela Parrott, Ristorante Siena
for
Piper Sonoma

Linguini with White Clam Sauce

3 cloves garlic, crushed
6 tablespoons olive oil
1/3 cup Sauvignon Blanc
3/4 cup fresh parsley, finely
 chopped

1 cup minced clams with
 liquid (or 4 cans clams with
 liquid)
1/8 teaspoon oregano
8 ounces linguini
12 hard shell clams
Grated Romano cheese

Saute garlic in the olive oil until golden (do not brown). Stir in 1 tablespoon flour and stir until smooth. Gradually add Sauvignon Blanc, parsley, clams with their liquid and oregano. Cook, stirring constantly, over medium heat until sauce is thickened and smooth. Add salt and pepper to taste.

Serve sauce over linguini and top with steamed hard shell clams and freshly grated Romano cheese.

Wine recommendation: Kunde Estate Sauvignon Blanc.

Marcia Kunde Mickelson
Kunde Estate Winery

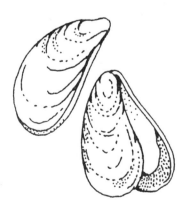
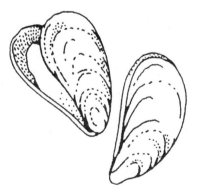

POULTRY

Green Olive Chicken

4 boneless chicken breasts,
 skinned and pounded
1/2 stick of butter
4 tablespoons olive oil
1/2 cup flour
1 teaspoon salt
1 teaspoon pepper
1/8 teaspoon Cayenne

2/3 cup stuffed green olives,
 sliced
1 cup yellow onions, chopped
10 halves sundried tomatoes
 in olive oil, drained
1 cup Fumé Blanc wine
3/4 cup half & half
2 large cloves garlic, finely
 minced

Mix flour, salt, cayenne and pepper in plastic bag. Add prepared chicken breasts. Shake to coat well. Meanwhile, heat butter and olive oil in a heavy skillet. Saute chicken until golden brown on both sides. Add wine, cover and simmer for 1 minute. Remove chicken, keep warm, add olives and onions to skillet and saute until onions are clear and tender. Add half & half, garlic and sundried tomatoes. Reduce by one half, stir often.

Pour 3/4 of the sauce on warm platter. Arrange chicken breasts. Pour remaining sauce over breasts. Serves four.

Serve with a crusty French bread, a green salad and Dry Creek Vineyard Fumé Blanc.

Brad Wallace
for
Dry Creek Vineyard

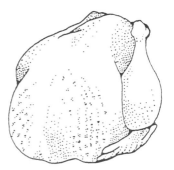

Herbed Game Birds in Red Wine

4 1-pound oven-ready young
  partridges, baby pheasants, quail
  or game hens
Salt
Freshly ground black pepper
1 cup flour
6 tablespoons unsalted butter
1/4 cup finely chopped shallots
2 cups (1/2 pound) thinly sliced
  mushrooms

2 tablespoons finely chopped
  cooked ham
2 cups dry red wine
2 tablespoons brandy
1 tablespoon fresh thyme
1 tablespoon fresh tarragon
1 small bay leaf
1 pinch ground nutmeg
2 tablespoons finely chopped
  parsley

Rinse the birds quickly under cold tap water and dry them inside and out with paper towels. Season them generously with salt and pepper, roll them in flour, then shake off the excess. In a heavy skillet, melt 3 tablespoons of the butter over moderate heat. Brown the birds on all sides, turning frequently. Remove and set aside.

Add one more tablespoon of the butter to skillet. Add 3 tablespoons of the shallots and cook, stirring, for 2 to 3 minutes. Add mushrooms and ham and cook, stirring for 2 to 3 more minutes until the mushrooms are golden brown. Transfer the mixture to a bowl and set aside.

Melt the remaining 2 tablespoons butter in the skillet and cook the remaining 1 tablespoon shallots for 2 to 3 minutes, until soft. Add the wine and brandy and bring to a boil over high heat, scraping up any brown bits from the bottom and sides of the pan. Add the thyme, tarragon, bay leaf, nutmeg, 1/2 teaspoon salt and black pepper to taste, then return the birds to the skillet.

Baste the birds thoroughly, reduce the heat to low, cover and simmer for 20 to 30 minutes, or until the birds are tender. Test by pressing a drumstick with your finger; it should show no resistance when the bird is fully cooked. Transfer the birds to a heated platter and cover them with foil, letting them rest while you prepare the sauce.

Bring the remaining pan juices to a brisk boil until the liquid is reduced to about one cup. Remove the bay leaf, stir in the mushroom/ham mixture and simmer for 1 to 2 minutes. Taste for seasoning and stir in the parsley. Serve the sauce on the side. Serves 4.

Serve with Sattui 1988 Suzanne's Vineyard Zinfandel.

Robert O'Malley, Operations Manager
V. Sattui Winery

Breast of Chicken a la Herbs

6 half chicken breasts
1 tablespoon each finely chopped
 basil, oregano and rosemary
1/4 cup flour
1 1/2 teaspoons salt
1/4 teaspoon pepper

1 tablespoon butter
2 tablespoons olive oil
1/2 cup chopped green
 onions
1/2 cup sliced mushrooms
1/2 cup Fumé Blanc

Bone 6 half chicken breasts.

Sprinkle with finely chopped basil, oregano and rosemary. Dredge with flour, salt and pepper. Lightly saute until brown in 1 tablespoon butter and 2 tablespoons olive oil for about 7 minutes. Turn once. Add 1/2 cup chopped green onions, 1/2 cup sliced mushrooms and saute three minutes. Add 1/2 cup Fumé Blanc. Simmer, covered, for 10 minutes.

Can be served with pasta or rice.

Serve with J. Pedroncelli Fumé Blanc.

Christine Pedroncelli
J. Pedroncelli Winery

Duck Breast with Black Currant Vinegar Sauce

DUCK BREASTS:

4 duck breasts, halved
Salt and freshly ground black
 pepper to taste

2 teaspoons fresh thyme
 leaves, chopped

Remove skin from duck and render a few pieces of the excess duck fat. When the fat is rendered, discard the crisp brown pieces of fat that remain.

Heat the rendered duck fat (enough to lightly coat the bottom of a large saute pan) and add the duck breasts. After 4 minutes, turn the breast over and cook for about 4 more minutes, or until just pink in the center of the breast. Allow to rest 5 minutes before carving.

BLACK CURRANT VINEGAR SAUCE:

3 shallots, chopped
1 medium carrot, chopped
1 cup reduced duck stock
4 sprigs fresh thyme
2 bay leaves

10 whole black peppercorns
3/4 cup black currant vinegar
1/2 cup dried black currants
Salt, to taste

In a saute pan, combine shallots, carrot, duck stock, thyme, bay leaves and peppercorns and reduce to half. Add vinegar and cook until reduced to about 3/4 cup. Add black currants and cook for 1 minute. Adjust seasoning.

Slice each duck breast in 4 to 5 slices and fan each breast, drizzling with the vinegar sauce. Serve with wild rice with pecans, and sauteed sweet potatoes. Serves 8.

Wine suggestion: Rodney Strong Vineyards Alexander's Crown Cabernet Sauvignon.

Bea Beasley
for
Rodney Strong Vineyards

Glazed Cornish Hens with Merlot Sauce

4 game hens

STUFFING:

2 1/3 cups chicken broth
1/2 cup wild rice
1/2 cup brown rice
2 tablespoons butter
1/2 cup chopped pecans
1 medium onion, diced

8 ounces sliced fresh
 mushrooms
1/4 cup chopped celery
2 tablespoons chopped fresh
 parsley
1/4 teaspoon thyme
Salt and Pepper

GLAZE:

2 tablespoons butter
1/2 cup raspberry jelly

2 tablespoons lemon juice
1/4 cup Merlot wine

Bring glaze ingredients to a boil and reduce. Set aside.

In medium saucepan, bring chicken broth to a boil. Add wild rice and butter. Cover and cook on low heat for 12 to 14 minutes. Add brown rice, cover and continue cooking for 45 minutes more or until all liquid is absorbed. Add 1 tablespoon butter and fluff with a fork. Saute onions, mushrooms and celery in 2 tablespoons butter until onions are transparent and celery is limp. Add to the cooked rice along with pecans, parsley, thyme, salt and pepper.

Preheat oven to 350 degrees.

Stuff hens with rice mixture. There will be extra, so put in a greased casserole the last 45 minutes and heat with the game hens. Bake hens for 1 1/2 hours, basting frequently with glaze. When done, remove hens from pan and pour off grease reserving pan juices for gravy. Stir in cornstarch and water mixture into pan for thickening gravy.

Serve with St. Francis Merlot.

Penny Cassina and Terrye Temple
for
St. Francis Vineyards & Winery

Orange Champagne Roasted Chicken
with Potato-Celeryroot Puree

3-4 pound roasting chicken, cut
into 8-10 pieces
2 valencia oranges, or other juice
orange, cut into 8 pieces

1/2 cup dry sparkling wine
Salt and pepper to taste

Place the chicken pieces is a 2-inch deep roasting pan, skin side up. Pour the sparkling wine over the chicken. Squeeze each orange section over the chicken and place the remaining rinds in the pan with the chicken. Season with salt and black pepper.

Place in a 375 degree oven for 50 minutes. Remove the juices from orange rinds from the pan and discard. Strain the juices into a saucepan, and de-grease. Then, bring to a boil and reduce by 1/2 volume. (Thicken slightly with corn starch if desired.)

Place the pan with the chicken pieces under a hot broiler to crisp the skin. Watch carefully so the skin does not burn.

POTATO-CELERYROOT PUREE:

2 large russet potatoes, peeled and
cut into 2-inch pieces
1 medium celeryroot, peeled and
cut into 2-inch pieces
1/2 cup heavy cream

1/4 cup unsalted butter
Salt and black pepper to taste
2 tablespoons orange rind,
finely chopped

Place the potatoes and celeryroot in a saucepan with enough water to cover the vegetables. Place over high heat and bring the water to a boil. Reduce the heat to a simmer and cook until tender. Heat the cream and the butter in a saucepan until the butter is melted. Drain the potatoes and celeryroot, then pass through a food mill. Quickly fold in the hot cream mixture and the orange rind. Season with salt and black pepper.

TO SERVE THIS DISH:

Spoon a portion of the potato puree in the center of each warmed plate. Place 1-2 pieces of chicken on the potato puree, then ladle some of the sauce (from the roasted chicken) over each portion. Serve with roasted or steamed green beans. Delicious!! Serves 4.

Serve with Mumm Cuvée Napa 1986 Winery Lake Sparkling Wine.

Elaine Bell
for
Mumm Cuvée Napa

Drunken Chicken

1 2-1/2 pound chicken
4 ounces balsamic vinegar
4 ounces Cabernet
2 ounces virgin olive oil
4 cloves fresh garlic, chopped

1/2 tablespoon fresh oregano
1 tablespoon each chopped
fresh basil, rosemary and
parsley
Salt and pepper to taste

Cut chicken into eight pieces. Mix remaining ingredients. Marinate chicken in mixture overnight. Take out chicken, place in pan. Broil until dark, approximately 15 minutes.

Place into baking dish. Add the marinade and bake at 450 degrees for 1/2 hour. Serve immediately.

Serve with J. Lohr Estates Seven Oaks Cabernet.

Chef Victor Rallo
for
J. Lohr Winery

Portuguese Chicken and Onions

6 boneless chicken thighs, cut
  into 3/4-inch cubes
2 medium yellow onions, cut in 1/2
  and sliced thin
1/2 cup Gamay Beaujolais
2 12-ounce cans chopped
  tomatoes in juice
1 bay leaf

1 1/2 teaspoons saffron
  powder
3 tablespoons flat leaf parsley,
  chopped
Salt
Pepper
Canola oil

In a large skillet, saute the chicken cubes over medium high heat in 2 tablespoons canola oil. Remove from the pan and set aside.

In the same pan, heat 2 tablespoons canola oil over medium heat and cook the onions until softened and translucent. Add the wine and reduce almost completely.

Pour complete contents of the tomato cans into the pan, then add the bay leaf and saffron. Simmer gently for 20 minutes.

Add the chicken and simmer an additional five minutes. Season with salt, pepper and parsley.

Serve over cooked rice or fusilli pasta. Serves 6.

Enjoy with a bottle of Beringer Gamay Beaujolais.

**Kerry Romaniello, Sous Chef
Beringer Vineyards**

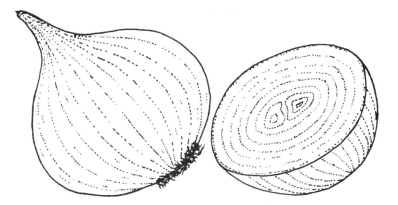

Baked Cornish Game Hens

4 Cornish game hens
2-3 tablespoons olive oil
1 teaspoon powdered cumin
Salt and pepper to taste

4 garlic cloves, peeled
6 sprigs fresh rosemary
1 cup Zinfandel

Preheat oven to 350 degrees. Sprinkle game hens with cumin, salt and pepper. Heat oil in an 8-quart Dutch oven. Add game hens and garlic, and brown over moderate heat for approximately 10 minutes. When birds are nicely brown, add rosemary. Cover the pot and place in oven for 45 minutes to 1 hour, or until birds are done.

Remove game hens and keep warm, discard the rosemary. Skim fat from the juices in pot. Mash soft garlic cloves and de-glaze the juices with Zinfandel. Increase heat and reduce liquid to about 2/3 of original volume.

To serve, place each hen on an individual plate and spoon some sauce over it. Serve with polenta or buttered noodles. Peas or snow peas will complete the meal.

Serve this with our Ravenswood Sonoma County Zinfandel.

Joel Peterson, Winemaker
Ravenswood Winery

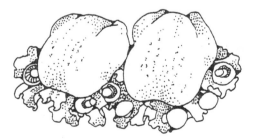

Chicken Charmoula

6 half chicken breasts, skinned and boned
1 clove garlic (about 1 teaspoon) minced
2 tablespoons Italian (flat leaf) parsley, chopped
2 tablespoons cilantro, chopped
1 teaspoon salt

3 teaspoons ground cumin
3 teaspoons sweet paprika
1/2 teaspoon Cayenne pepper
4 tablespoons lemon juice
4 tablespoons olive oil
1 cup homemade or good commercial mayonnaise*
Cilantro sprigs for garnish

This recipe was inspired by a traditional Moroccan seasoning. Arrange chicken in a glass or ceramic dish. Mince garlic in food processor fitted with steel blade. Add all remaining herbs and spices and process. Add lemon juice and olive oil and puree. Spread half the spice mixture over all surfaces of chicken. Cover and marinate, refrigerated, 2 to 12 hours. Refrigerate balance of spice mixture.

Prepare fire in grill or heat broiler. Grill or broil chicken about 3 minutes per side. Meanwhile, mix reserved spice mixture with the mayonnaise to make sauce.

Serve each piece of chicken with a dollop of sauce, garnished with cilantro springs. This dish is equally enjoyable served hot or at room temperature. Serves 4 to 6.

* The diet conscious will find a squeeze of lemon a very satisfying substitute for the mayonnaise sauce.

Mary Evely, Chef
Simi Winery

Sausage, Apple and Apricot Stuffing

Serve with turkey or small game birds, such as squab or pheasant.

2 cups finely chopped yellow onion
1 cup chopped celery
6 tablespoons butter
1 pound chorizo or other spicy sausage, cut into 1/4 inch cubes
8 cups wheatberry or other whole-grain bread, 1/2 inch cubes and oven toasted

1 cup peeled and diced tart apples
1 cup diced dried apricots
1/2 cup minced fresh parsley
2 teaspoons fresh oregano (or 1 teaspoon dried)
1/2-1 cup chicken stock (as needed)

Preheat oven to 325 degrees. In a large skillet, saute onions and celery in butter until onions are translucent. Add sausage, saute 4 to 5 minutes. Remove from heat. In a large bowl, combine mixture with remaining ingredients except stock. Mix thoroughly. Gradually add stock until mixture is moist, but still light and loose.

Place stuffing in a lightly buttered oven-proof casserole and bake, covered, until the edges are lightly browned and slightly crisp, 1 to 1-1/2 hours. Remove cover for the last 15 to 20 minutes. Serves 8 to 10.

Recommended wine: Fetzer Oaks Cabernet Sauvignon or Fetzer Gewurztraminer. The stuffing is nicely underscored by the luscious, engaging fruit of the Valley Oaks Cabernet Sauvignon. The Gewurztraminer is a spicy, slightly sweet white wine option.

John Ash, Culinary Director
Fetzer Vineyards

John Ash, one of California's most influential chefs, helped to nurture a cuisine that has become international, in its usage of fresh, seasonal ingredients of the region of the chef. As Executive Chef of John Ash and Co., his own restaurant, he won countless awards for his innovative recipes. Now the Culinary Director for Fetzer Vineyards, he is heading the winery's food and wine educational program, nationally and internationally.

Rosemary Chicken and Mushrooms

6 boned chicken breast halves, skinned (pounded to 1/4-inch thickness)
1 tablespoon each butter and olive oil
2-3 cloves fresh garlic, minced

2 cups fresh mushrooms, sliced
1/2 cup white wine
1/2 cup lemon juice
2 teaspoons fresh rosemary, minced
Salt and pepper to taste

Saute garlic, mushrooms and rosemary in oil/butter combination, then cover pan and simmer over low heat about 2 to 3 minutes, until mushrooms are tender.

Strain mixture and set mushrooms aside, then use seasoned butter to brown chicken breasts (approximately 2 to 3 minutes on each side over medium-high heat).

Return mushrooms to pan with chicken, add lemon juice and wine and simmer, covered, for 5 to 7 minutes. Remove lid and continue cooking 2 minutes longer to reduce liquid.

To serve, top chicken breasts with mushroom mixture, garnish with fresh parsley or sprig of fresh rosemary.

Recommended wine: Lake Sonoma Winery 1989 Sauvignon Blanc.

Kate Moore
for
Lake Sonoma Winery

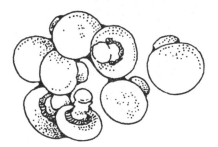

Chicken Breast with Raspberry Sauce

6 chicken breast halves, skinned
 and boned
4 tablespoons butter
1 medium onion, coarsely chopped
2 cloves garlic, minced
1/2 cup Raspberry Wine
2 tablespoons white wine vinegar

1/2 cup chicken stock
1/2 cup heavy cream
1 small tomato, peeled,
 seeded and chopped
1/2 pint fresh raspberries
Salt and pepper to taste

Flatten chicken breast to half the original thickness. Melt butter in a large skillet and brown chicken on both sides over moderate heat. Remove and set aside. Add onions and garlic to skillet and cook until tender, 8 to 10 minutes. Add wine and vinegar and bring to a boil, stirring constantly. Reduce liquid to about two tablespoons. Add chicken stock, cream and tomatoes and whisk for a minute or two.

Return chicken to pan and simmer until chicken is hot and sauce is reduced by half, 5 minutes or so. Remove chicken to warm platter.

Add raspberries to sauce, swirling them around by shaking the skillet. Salt and pepper to taste and pour over chicken breast. Serves 6.

The finishing touch to this dish is our rich, fruity Pinot Noir.

**Patricia Ballard, Senior Wine Counselor
Bargetto Winery**

Annamaria Roudon's Chicken with Wine

1 medium size chicken, cut in
 serving size pieces
5 slices bacon
20 small mushrooms
2 cups Petite Sirah
1 medium carrot, chopped
4 whole cloves
2 sprigs fresh rosemary

4 sprigs fresh thyme
20 small onions
2 tablespoons olive oil
2 cups chicken broth
4 bay leaves
4 sprigs fresh oregano
Salt and pepper to taste

Preheat oven to 350 degrees. Cut bacon into small pieces and brown in deep iron pot or a dutch oven. Remove and set aside. Add the olive oil, brown the chicken pieces on all sides, remove and set aside.

Saute the onions and mushrooms in the remaining oil until the onions are just transparent, remove and set aside. Add the Petite Sirah and the chicken broth, and boil over high heat until the liquid is reduced to about 3 cups. Reduce the heat and return all the reserved ingredients to the pan. Add the carrot, cloves, oregano, bay leaves, rosemary and thyme. Cover and bake in oven at 350 degrees for about 1 hour or until chicken is done.

Serve hot in shallow serving dish or in individual ramekins. Serves 4.

Serve with Roudon-Smith Petite Sirah.

Annamaria Roudon
Roudon Smith Vineyards

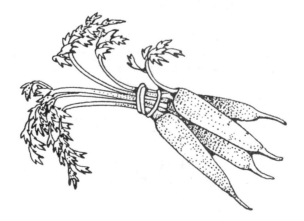

Violet's Lemon Chicken

4 half chicken breasts, skinned
1 large red bell pepper, sliced
1/2 pound mushrooms, quartered
1 small jar marinated artichokes,
 drained and quartered
1 head of garlic, cloves peeled
 and halved
Juice of 4 lemons

Fumé Blanc
Olive oil
Salt
Lemon pepper seasoning
Fresh chopped cilantro
Fresh chopped basil
Fresh chopped parsley

Optional: Sugar peas, cucumber, celery, green apples. May be added to vegetable saute.

Marinate the chicken breasts at least two hours with half the garlic, the juice of 2 lemons and enough wine to barely cover.

Remove the chicken breasts from the marinade and pat dry. Season with salt and lemon pepper. Heat a saute pan. Add a thin layer of olive oil and the remaining half of the garlic, being careful not to over brown. Add the chicken breasts and saute until nicely browned, turning once. Remove to a hot oven and keep warm, covered.

Add the juice of the remaining two lemons to the pan with a cup of the wine. Boil to reduce by half and reserve.

Saute the vegetables in a little olive oil, as above, beginning with the bell pepper and continuing in order. Cook only until crisp tender. Remove to the oven and keep warm.

Return the reduced liquid to the pan and reheat. Season to taste with salt and lemon pepper.

Arrange the chicken breasts on a serving plate surrounded with the vegetables. Sprinkle with the chopped fresh herbs. Serves 4.

This recipe brings together the flavors most complimentary to Grgich Hills Fumé Blanc - lemon, pepper, herbs and garlic.

Violet Grgich
Grgich Hills Cellar

Poulet Japonaise

1/4 cup melted margarine
1/4 cup Dijon mustard

2 cloves garlic

PANKO MIXTURE:

2 tablespoons grated Parmesan
cheese
1 cup Panko Japanese bread
crumbs*

1 tablespoon minced parsley
6 boneless, skinless chicken
breasts

DIJON SAUCE:

1/4 cup mayonnaise
1/4 cup yogurt

1/4 cup Dijon mustard
2 scallions, minced

Combine melted margarine with mustard and garlic and turn chicken breasts in this marinade, coating them completely. Dip and coat each breast in the panko mixture. Place in 8X13-inch rimmed baking pan, and bake in middle of preheated oven at 500 degrees for 15 minutes. Cut crosswise into 1-inch slices, and arrange on plates, with a dollop of the sauce. Garnish the slices with thinly sliced whites from scallions.

*Available from Japanese section in food markets.

Delightful served with rice and fresh asparagus, and paired with a light and dry Sauvignon Blanc.

Duane Bue

Duane Bue, a realtor in Santa Rosa, is one of the many highly creative chefs in this region. This recipe is one of his favorites...and one of ours. VMH

Turkey Steaks in Peanut Sauce

6-8 turkey steaks, or
6-8 chicken breasts

MARINADE:

1/2 cup chunky peanut butter
1/4 cup sesame oil
1/4 cup peanut oil
1/4 cup soy sauce
1/4 cup rice wine vinegar
1/4 cup lemon juice

3 cloves garlic, minced
1/4 cup chopped cilantro
2 teaspoons chopped fresh
 ginger
2 teaspoons dried red pepper
 flakes

Combine all of the above ingredients. A food processor works best.
If marinade is too thick, it can be thinned with about 1/2 cup white
wine or water.

Marinate 6 to 8 turkey steaks (or chicken breasts) all day or overnight.
Grill over hot coals for 10 minutes on each side, basting with remaining
marinade. Serve with grilled fresh vegetables. Serves 6 to 8.

Goes great with De Loach Vineyards Early Harvest Gewurztraminer.

Michael Shafer, Executive Chef of Chez Melange
for
De Loach Vineyards

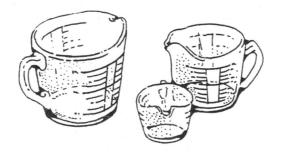

Apple-Ginger Chutney

Serve with unseasoned chicken breasts, grilled, sauteed or broiled.

4 ounces (1 stick) unsalted butter
4 apples (Granny Smith or other
 tart, firm variety) peeled and
 coarsely chopped
2 tablespoons apple juice
2 tablespoons orange juice
2 tablespoons lemon juice

2 teaspoons orange zest,
 grated
1 tablespoon fresh ginger,
 pressed through garlic press
 (about 1-inch piece, peeled)
1/3 cup pistachios, shelled,
 skinned and chopped

In butter, saute apples over medium heat, stirring frequently, until pieces are golden outside and tender inside. Add apple, orange and lemon juices when apples begin to get tender. Stir in orange zest and ginger; cook briefly to blend flavors. Add salt if necessary. Just before serving, top with chopped pistachios. Makes 2 cups, serves 8.

This recipe was developed for Kendall-Jackson Vintner's Reserve Chardonnay. This medium-bodied wine is full of citrus, melon and tropical fruit, along with buttery and honey flavors.

Kendall-Jackson Vineyard

Chardonnay Chicken Marinade

2 cups Chardonnay
2 sprigs rosemary, broken up
3/4 cup oil
4 large garlic cloves, cut coarsely
1 tablespoon Worcestershire sauce
Paprika

1/4 cup ketchup
1/4 cup barbecue sauce, any
 brand
Salt and pepper
Italian seasoning

Pour over chicken. For best results, let stand for several hours or even overnight. Serve with a Chardonnay or a White Zinfandel from Sausal.

Roselee Demonstene & Cindy Martin, Co-Owners
Sausal Winery

Chicken en Casserole

4 pounds cut-up young chicken
1/2 pound raw, lean ham slice
2 medium size onions
3 carrots
1 cup Merlot
1/2 cup chicken stock
4 tablespoons olive oil
3 tablespoons margarine or butter

1 clove garlic, mashed
1 teaspoon cloves
1 teaspoon tarragon
1 bay leaf
Pinch of thyme
Pinch of marjoram
Salt and pepper

Pat chicken pieces dry and season them with a mix of salt, pepper, thyme and marjoram. Heat olive oil to smoking in a casserole, add the chicken pieces and brown them evenly, turning frequently. Drain off the olive oil.

In a separate bowl, place the butter mixed with the tarragon, the ham cut into thin strips, the carrots scraped and sliced, the onions sliced thinly, the bay leaf, cloves, garlic, the red wine and chicken stock. Mix thoroughly and add to the chicken in the casserole dish.

Cover and cook over low flame for 45 minutes, turning it twice during the cooking. Serves 6 to 8.

Serve with Conn Creek 1989 Napa Valley Merlot.

Conn Creek Winery

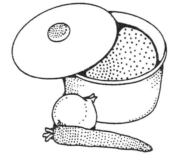

Late Harvest Game Hens
with Croissant Stuffing

12 day-old croissants, pulled apart
1 cup yellow raisins
3/4 cup sliced almonds
1-2 cups poultry stock
1 cube unsalted sweet butter
1 tablespoon poultry seasoning
6 Cornish game hens
Salt and pepper

2 medium apples, cored and
 diced
1 medium yellow onion, diced
5 stalks celery, diced
1 large egg, beaten
1 cup water
1/2 tablespoon cinnamon
1 bottle Chardonnay

Clean and pat dry Cornish game hens, set aside. Combine egg, croissants, raisins, almonds, onions, celery, apple, poultry seasoning and cinnamon in a bowl. Add stock a little at a time until the mixture takes on a sticky dressing-like consistency. Salt and pepper to taste.

Rub hens with butter and stuff hens with the above mixture. Set hens in a long, foil-lined baking pan. Pour Chardonnay over the hens. Add water to the bottom of the pan, as needed. Salt and pepper hens to taste. Bake uncovered at 350 degrees for 1 hour, basting every 15 minutes. Garnish with orange slices and fresh peppermint leaves. Serves 6.

Serve with Beaucanon Late Harvest Chardonnay.

**Deborah Thorman, Hospitality Director
Beaucanon Winery**

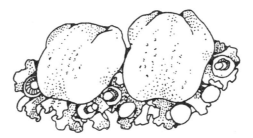

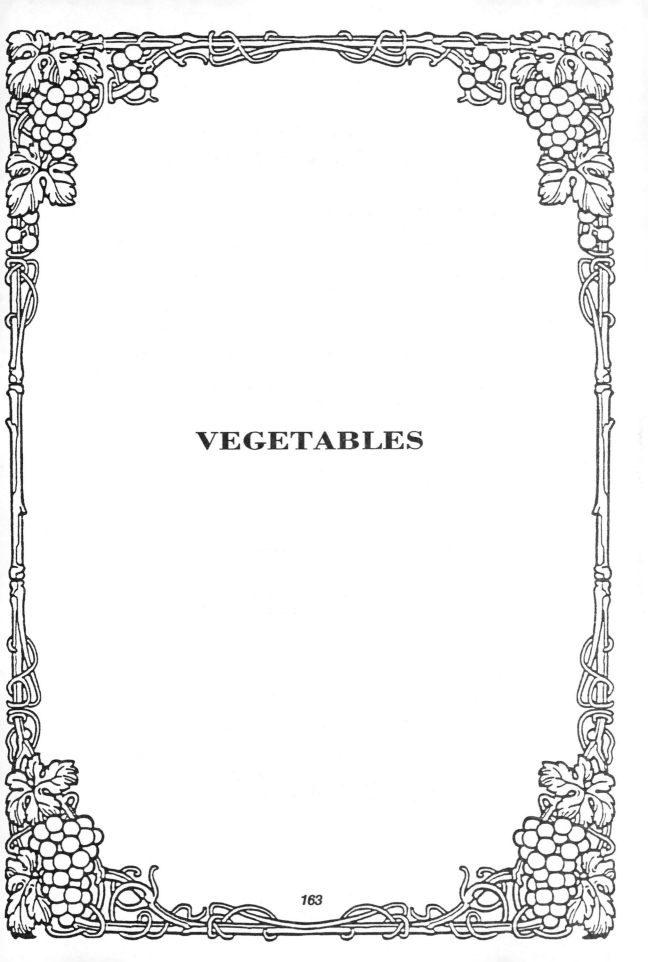

VEGETABLES

Broiled Ratatouille Vegetables with Penne

1 medium eggplant
Salt
2 large red bell peppers, roasted
(see note)
4 medium tomatoes
1/2 cup olive oil
8 ounces penne, cooked al dente
3 tablespoons red wine vinegar

1 tablespoon minced shallot
1 medium garlic clove, finely
chopped
Freshly ground pepper to
taste
1 tablespoon minced fresh
parsley
1/4 cup basil, chopped

Wash and dry the eggplant, cut off the top, and cut into 1/4-inch slices. Sprinkle with salt and set in a colander over a plate. Allow to drain for 30 minutes.

Cut pepper in half lengthwise. Drain on paper towels.

Cut tomatoes in half horizontally and remove seeds. Put them on a baking sheet, cut side up, and broil until they begin to brown, about 5 minutes or less. Set aside.

Rinse or pat off salt from eggplant and brush with olive oil on both sides. Broil until golden on both sides, several minutes.

Cut cooked eggplant into strips and tomatoes into large chunks. Place in a mixing bowl. Add peppers and toss. Add vegetables to cooked penne. Pour vinegar, remaining olive oil, shallots and garlic over all. Toss and season to taste with salt and freshly ground black pepper. Sprinkle with parsley and basil before serving. Serve hot or at room temperature. Serves 8.

NOTE: To peel peppers, char them over a gas flame or under the broiler until blackened on all sides. Place the peppers in a paper bag and fold closed. Allow to sit for approximately 15 minutes, then peel and seed under running water. Drain well on paper towels.

Annie Roberts, Chef, The Vineyard Room
Robert Mondavi Winery

Asparagus with Sauteed Fennel and Red Bell Pepper Sauce

2 pounds fresh asparagus
3 tablespoons sugar
1/2 fresh fennel bulb

2-3 tablespoons unsweetened
butter

Make Red Bell Pepper Sauce first and reserve over a warm water bath.

Snap stiff ends from asparagus and wash stalks; drain. Wash fennel bulb, snipping feathery tips and reserving them for garnish. Slice the bulb in narrow slices as you would celery stalks. (Fennel can also be rubbed with oil and grilled, then sliced.)

Caramelize the sugar in the bottom of a heavy skillet while boiling water in a tea kettle. When sugar is completely melted, place asparagus on top of the sugar. Salt and pepper, and cover immediately with boiling water. Cook for 8 to 12 minutes, or until asparagus is done but still retains its fresh green color. Drain immediately.

While the asparagus is cooking, melt butter in a pan and saute fennel slices until almost translucent. Ground fennel seed can be added.

RED BELL PEPPER SAUCE:

2 tablespoons fresh marjoram or
 chopped parsley
1/2 cup Fumé Blanc
2 tablespoons lemon juice

4 tablespoons minced shallots
2 red bell peppers, chopped
1 cube unsalted butter,
 softened

Simmer shallots, lemon juice and wine together in a saucepan for 10 minutes to volatilize the alcohol and reduce the volume to half the original liquid amount. Core, seed and chop the red bell peppers and put into a blender and puree with the herbs. Add the reduced shallot/wine mixture and blend. Return to saucepan and heat to a simmer. Slowly whisk in the butter, one tablespoon at a time, to build an emulsion. Can be held over tepid water until served or can be kept in a glass container, covered until used.

PRESENTATION:

Arrange the asparagus spears on a plate and drape with sauteed fennel; spoon Red Bell Pepper Sauce down the center and serve immediately. Garnish with snipped fennel sprigs. Serves 4 to 6.

Fresh, tender asparagus is a favorite vegetable. However, its oxalic acids can be very "unfriendly" to most wines. You'll find it is a perfect match for McDowell Fumé Blanc when grilled or combined with sauteed fennel and red bell pepper sauce.

Karen Keehn, Proprietor
McDowell Valley Vineyards

Baked Cauliflower
in Tomato Cheese Sauce

1 medium cauliflower, whole
2 cups stewed tomatoes
1 grated onion
Lemon
Salt and pepper to taste

1/2 cup grated Parmesan
 cheese
1 cup bread crumbs
1 tablespoon butter

Blanch cauliflower head in water with lemon juice. Cook until crisp tender. Don't overcook. Drain well. Place in baking dish, head up. Add grated onion to tomatoes. Pour over cauliflower.

Combine crumbs and cheese and sprinkle over cauliflower. Dot with 1 tablespoon of butter. Salt and pepper to taste. Bake in a 375 degree oven until golden and browned. Serves 4 to 6.

Conn Creek Winery

Sweet Corn Pie

8 ears of corn	1 hard-boiled egg, cut in
1 cup of milk	wedges
1 tablespoon butter	4 egg yolks
1 tablespoon flour	1 teaspoon confectioners
4 egg whites	sugar
20 black olives	1 1/2 pounds ground beef
1/2 cup raisins	1 large onion, chopped
	Cumin, oregano, salt, pepper

Saute onion until transparent, add the meat and saute until cooked. Add raisins, the hard boiled egg, salt, pepper, oregano, cumin and olives. This preparation is called "Pino." If you like your food spicy, add a few drops of chili sauce or serve with picante sauce. Grind the corn kernels. Cook with the butter, flour and milk in a heavy pan, stirring continuously. Remove from heat. Beat the egg yolks and add to the corn mixture. Whip the egg whites until they are stiff and fold into corn mixture. Arrange the "Pino" in a baking dish or in individual ramekins and cover it with the corn mixture. Spread a little sugar on top and bake in a 350 degree oven until golden. Serves 6.

Clos Du Val winemaker, Bernard Portet, says "I am a beast in the kitchen, and learned my love and appreciation of fine food from my mother, my wife and other fine chefs." This delicious Chilean dish comes from his wife, Helia. It is delightful as a main course at dinner or for a luncheon. Serve piping hot from the oven with a mixed green salad or a tomato, onion and cilantro salad - very Chilean! Enjoy a glass of Clos Du Val Chardonnay or Pinot Noir with this wonderful Sweet Corn Pie!

Mrs. Bernard Portet
Clos Du Val Winery

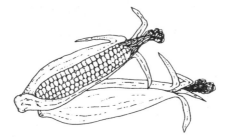

Colcannon

1 pound white cabbage (after core
is removed)
1 teaspoon salt
3 pounds potatoes, scrubbed and
sliced with skins left on
4 medium leeks, thoroughly
washed and sliced

1 cup milk
1/2 teaspoon mace
Salt and pepper to taste
4 garlic cloves
8 tablespoons butter (1 stick)

Bring a pot of salted water to a boil, and boil the cabbage until tender, about 12 to 15 minutes. Drain off the water and chop the cabbage. Set aside. Bring another pot of water to a boil and boil the potatoes until tender. Drain off the water and set aside. Put the leeks in a saucepan, cover with milk, and bring close to boiling, and then turn down to a simmer until tender. Set aside.

Add the mace, salt and pepper, and garlic to the pot with the potatoes and mash them well with a hand masher. Now add the leeks and their milk and mix in with the potatoes, taking care, however (for the sake of texture), not to break the leeks down too much. Add a little more milk if necessary to make it smooth. Now mash in the cabbage, and lastly the butter. The texture that you want to achieve is a smooth-butter-potato with interesting pieces of leek and cabbage well distributed in it.

Transfer the whole mixture to an ovenproof dish, make a pattern on the surface, for example, the fork-furrow pattern, and place under the broiler to brown. Serves 6.

Serve with Concannon Vineyard Sauvignon Blanc.

Concannon Vineyard

This is a very, very old Irish recipe that the Concannon family brought with them from Ireland.

Pinto Bean Puree with Creme Frâiche

14 ounces pinto beans
1 large onion, 1/4-inch dice
1 large carrot, 1/4-inch dice
1 rib celery, 1/4-inch dice
6 cloves garlic, smashed
8 ounces tomatoes, seeded
2 jalapeno peppers, seeded
3 ounces Anaheim pepper, seeded
4 teaspoons cumin
4 teaspoons chili powder

1 teaspoon Cayenne pepper
1 ham hock
8 parsley stems
5 thyme sprigs
2 bay leaves
Tabasco to taste
8 cups chicken stock
0 ounces butter
10 teaspoons creme frâiche
(or sour cream)

Soak beans overnight, drain and then rinse. Using a thick-bottomed pan, melt butter and sweat the onions, carrots, celery, garlic and peppers. Add the spices and beans, stir. Add the stock and the rest of the ingredients. Bring to a boil and turn heat down to a simmer. Continue cooking the soup, stirring occasionally for 2 1/2 hours, or to the point when the beans are tender. To make easy straining, pass quickly at low speed through a blender, then strain.

Serve in a warm bowl. Place a teaspoon of creme frâiche (or sour cream) in the center. The creme frâiche may be flavored slightly with chopped oregano and a pinch of garlic. Serves 10.

Recommended wine: Chateau Souverain Sauvignon Blanc.

Martin W. Courtman, Executive Chef
Chateau Souverain

Summer Vegetable Ratatouille

2 medium-sized eggplants
2 medium-sized onions
2 large green peppers
4 large, peeled tomatoes
3 large zucchini
1/4 cup olive oil
4 cloves garlic

1 teaspoon each basil and
 thyme
1/2 teaspoon oregano
2 bay leaves
2 teaspoons salt
1/4 teaspoon pepper

Cut eggplant and zucchini into 1/2-inch slices, then cut into quarters. Sprinkle eggplant with one tablespoon salt; let stand while you prepare other vegetables. Chop the onions, peppers and tomatoes into large chunks. Rinse salt off eggplant; pat dry.

Pour olive oil in a 6-quart or large Dutch oven, and place over medium heat. Add the onions and peppers; cook, stirring until limp. Add zucchini and eggplant and cook, stirring occasionally until lightly browned. Stir in tomatoes and the spices. Bring to a boil; reduce heat, cover and simmer until vegetables are almost tender, about 20 to 30 minutes.

Remove cover and boil gently, stirring occasionally, until most of the liquid evaporates, about 10 to 20 minutes longer. Cook, cover and chill. Makes 6 to 8 servings.

Serve with Peju Dry Rosé or Peju Chardonnay, Napa Valley.

Herta Peju, Owner
Peju Province Winery

Mushroom-Eggplant Medley

2 small eggplants, cubed
1 cup thinly sliced onion
1 clove garlic, mashed
3 large tomatoes, peeled and
 chopped
1/2 pound mushrooms, sliced

1/2 teaspoon ground cloves
1 teaspoon chili powder
1/2 teaspoon ground
 coriander
Salt and pepper to taste
4 tablespoons oil

Heat oven to 350 degrees.

Saute eggplant, 1/2 at a time, browning lightly. Drain on paper. Saute onions, garlic and mushrooms, browning lightly. Add tomatoes, chili powder, coriander, cloves, salt and pepper. Simmer for 10 minutes. Add eggplant and mix well.

Turn into a baking casserole. Top with a light dusting of bread crumbs and Parmesan cheese. Bake 35 to 40 minutes. Serves 4 to 6.

Serve with Landmark 1990 Sonoma County Chardonnay.

Landmark Vineyards

Corn Pudding

6 ears of corn, grated
6 tablespoons butter
1/2 teaspoon baking powder
3 eggs separated

1 teaspoon salt
1 teaspoon sugar
1 cup milk
1/2 green pepper, minced fine
1 teaspoon flour

Cream butter well, add beaten yolks of eggs, grated corn and other ingredients; add the egg whites, beaten stiff, last. Bake in slow oven at 325 degrees for 30 minutes or until set so that the pudding does not adhere to a knife of spoon inserted to test.

This is a very old wine country recipe that is still a favorite in some of our local restaurants.

Zucchini and Carrots

2 1/2 cups carrots
2 1/2 cups zucchini
2 tablespoons olive oil

1 clove garlic, crunched
1 tablespoon lemon juice
3 tablespoons sweet Vermouth

Cut the vegetables in julienne style. Use a large frying pan or wok, add oil to *hot* pan. Saute garlic and carrots for 2 minutes and then add zucchini. Toss about 2 minutes. Add lemon juice and wine. Toss about briefly, remove from heat and serve.

Jeani Martini
Martini & Pratti Wines

Broccoli Casserole

3 cups cooked short grain brown rice
1 pound mushrooms sliced or quartered, sauteed
1 large onion chopped and sauteed with 3 cloves minced garlic
2 1/2 cups shredded Jack cheese

2 cups basic white sauce
Splash of white wine
Salt and pepper
Basil
1 large bunch broccoli (about 3 cups) broken into flowerettes (peel and chop stems) parboiled and drained (or cauliflower)

Combine all ingredients and pour into baking dish. Top with toasted cashew pieces or sunflower seeds if desired. Bake, covered, for 30 minutes in preheated oven at 350 degrees. Uncover and bake 10 minutes more to a golden brown.

The Sonoma Cheese Factory

As served at the Sonoma Valley Vintners' Picnic in the Park.

Sauvignon Blanc
Rice Vegetable Casserole

1 cup chopped onions
1 pound lean hamburger
1 cup chopped greens from green
  onion
1/2 cup chopped chives
1 cup bean sprouts
1 cup white rice
1 teaspoon salt

1 teaspoon English thyme
1 teaspoon lemon thyme
1 teaspoon chopped parsley
1 teaspoon chopped tarragon
1 1/2 cups water
1/2 cup sauvignon blanc
Soy sauce to taste

Lightly saute onions with hamburger. Add chopped green onions, chives and bean sprouts. Saute with onions and hamburger. Add white rice. Toss rice with vegetables and ground beef. Allow rice to toast at low heat for 3 to 5 minutes. Stir gently to keep rice from sticking. Sprinkle mixture with salt. Add the herbs. Toss to distribute evenly.

Stir in water and wine. Cover and simmer over low heat for 30 minutes or until rice is tender. Season with soy sauce and serve with a garden salad and Guenoc Sauvignon Blanc. Serves 4 to 6.

At Guenoc, the Magoons use their own range-fed beef for this casserole. Chicken or turkey may be substituted, or the onions, rice and vegetables can be sauteed in a little olive oil for a meatless version. Brown or wild rice can also be substituted, but allow for a longer cooking time and additional water or wine.

Karen Melander-Magoon
Guenoc Winery

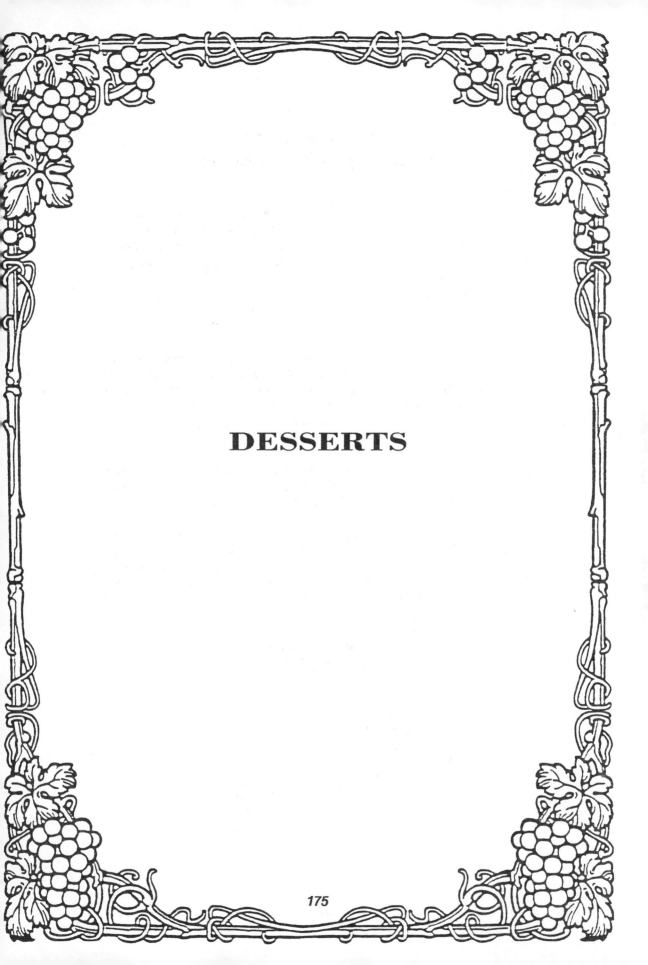

DESSERTS

Walter Raymond's Gold Medal Cheesecake

FILLING:

3 7-ounce packages cream cheese
2 eggs
3/4 cups, plus 1 tablespoon sugar
1 teaspoon vanilla

CRUST:

9 ounces graham cracker
  crumbs
3/4 cube butter, melted

Preheat oven to 375 degrees.

Prepare crust by mixing graham cracker crumbs with the melted butter. Using a 9 or 10-inch springform pan, press mixture onto bottom and sides of pan. Set aside.

Crumble the 3 packages of cream cheese into a mixing bowl and add the two eggs, one at a time. Beat well, until of a creamy consistency. Add the sugar and vanilla and beat again. Pour into the crust and bake for 20 minutes.

TOP LAYER:

3 small cartons sour cream
1 tablespoon sugar
1 teaspoon vanilla

TOPPING (OPTIONAL):

Your favorite fruit puree

While cake is in the oven, mix together the sour cream, sugar and vanilla. Quickly remove the cheesecake from the oven and cover with the sour cream mixture. Return to the oven for 5 minutes.

Remove from the oven, and place immediately into the refrigerator. Chill thoroughly before serving, overnight if desired.

Top with a fruit puree just before serving, if you like extra flavor and color.

Walter Raymond
Raymond Vineyards and Cellars

This recipe was voted as the "Best Dessert" at a local charity event called "Valley Men Who Cook." Walter has received many medals for his wine over the years, but this was the first medal for his baking!

Pear and Dried Cherry Crisp

FRUIT:

1 cup dried sour cherries
1/2 cup Brandy
8 firm pears, such as Bartlett or
 Bosc
Juice of one lemon
1/4 cup sugar
Pinch of cinnamon

TOPPING:

1 3/4 cup all purpose flour
2 cups walnuts or almonds
2/3 cup brown sugar
1/4 teaspoon cinnamon
2 tablespoons sugar
2/3 cup salted butter

Marinate cherries in Brandy (1/2 cup).

Lightly toast nuts in 350 degree oven for 10 minutes. Let cool.

For the topping, mix flour, sugars, cinnamon, and cut in butter with fingers until mixture is crumbly and has a streusel consistency.

Chop nuts, and combine with rest of topping mixture.

For fruit, peel, core and cut pears into 2-inch pieces. Marinate in 1/4 cup sugar, lemon juice and cinnamon.

Combine cherries and brandy into pear mixture. Spoon into heat-proof terracotta or Pyrex baking dish. Sprinkle crisp mixture over top.

Bake in 350 degree preheated oven for 40 to 45 minutes. Serve warm or at room temperature with creme frâiche, whipped cream or ice cream. Serves 6 to 8.

Best enjoyed while sipping Carneros Alambic Distillery's RMS Special Reserve Brandy.

Michele Mutrux
for
Carneros Alambic Distillery

Polenta Pudding with
Fresh Blackberry Compote and
"Petite Liqueur," Mascarpone Whipped Cream

1 cup polenta
2 cups bread flour
2 egg yolks
4 eggs

BERRY COMPOTE:

4 cups fresh blackberries
1/2 cup granulated sugar
1/4 cup "Petite Liqueur"

1/4 Tahitian vanilla bean
 (scrape inside)
5 cups powdered sugar
1 1/2 cups sweet butter

MASCARPONE CREAM:

4 ounces mascarpone
8 ounces whipping cream
1 1/2 ounces sugar
*all whipped to a soft peak

In an electric mixer, beat the softened butter, sugar and vanilla until creamy. Beat in the eggs and egg yolks one at a time. Fold in flour and polenta. Pour into 12-inch greased and floured cake pan. Bake 1 hour and 15 minutes in a preheated oven at 325 degrees. Unmold on a rack and let cool. Place cake in a larger size cake pan. Pour cooked berries and juices on top and around cake, cover and soak overnight. Cut cake into slices and garnish with mascarpone cream on top and a few fresh blackberries. Add a few drops of "Petite Liqueur," a mint tip and some of the berry juices around the cake. Serve at room temperature.

This elegant dessert marries well with Chandon Blanc de Noirs.

Philippe Jeanty, Chef de Cuisine
Domaine Chandon

Red Raspberry Crepes

1 4-ounce container whipped cream cheese
10 dessert crepes (see recipe)
3 tablespoons sugar
1 cup apple-raspberry cider
1 tablespoon butter or margarine
1 pint fresh raspberries or one 10-ounce package frozen, thawed and drained

2 tablespoons toasted slivered almonds
1 teaspoon cornstarch
1 teaspoon orange liqueur
1/4 cup toasted slivered almonds
1 tablespoon lemon juice

Spread cheese over uncrowned side of each dessert crepe, leaving 1/4 inch rim around edge. Sprinkle each crepe with a portion of the 2 tablespoons of almonds. Fold each crepe into a triangle by folding in half, then half again. Cover crepes, set aside. In a 10-inch skillet, combine the sugar, cornstarch, and dash salt. Stir in apple-raspberry cider and butter or margarine. Cook and stir 2 minutes more. Stir in liqueur, lemon juice and raspberries. Add crepes to sauce, heat through. Sprinkle the 1/4 cup almonds on top. Serve immediately. Serves 10.

CREPES:

1 cup flour
2 tablespoons sugar
1/8 teaspoon salt

2 eggs
1 1/2 cups milk
1/4 cup butter, melted

Beat with rotary beater until well mixed. Heat lightly greased 6-inch skillet, remove from heat. Spoon in 2 tablespoons of batter, lift and tilt skillet to spread thinly, return to heat. Do not turn over. Invert pan over paper towel to remove crepe. Repeat for other crepes. Makes 16.

Carol Kozlowski-Every
Kozlowski Farms

Orange Custard with
Strawberries and Muscat Canelli

2 cups milk
Slivered zest of 2 oranges
2 eggs
4 egg yolks
1/2 cup sugar

1 teaspoon vanilla
2 cups strawberries cut in half
1 375 ml. Muscat Canelli
6 custard cups

Preheat oven to 350 degrees. Scald milk with the orange zest. In large mixing bowl, beat the eggs and lightly stir in the sugar. Add the milk slowly, stirring constantly. Add the vanilla and blend well. Strain and pour into the cups. Place the cups in a shallow baking pan. Fill the pan with boiling water to 1/2 way up the sides of the cups. Bake in center of oven for about 35 minutes until the custard feels firm when pressed.

Remove from water, cool and chill in refrigerator for at least 2 hours. Meanwhile, put Muscat in small saucepan, bring to a boil and reduce to 1/4 cup or syrup consistency and chill. Toss with strawberries 1/2 hour before serving. Unmold custard onto individual plates.

Surround with strawberries and drizzle with the syrup that remains from the strawberries. Serve immediately. Serves 6.

You'll enjoy our Muscat Canelli with this.

Stella Fleming, Executive Chef
Glen Ellen Winery

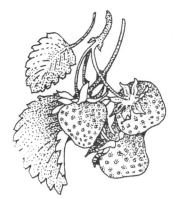

Bittersweet Chocolate Souffle

8 ounces bittersweet chocolate, in small chunks
1/3 cup strong coffee
2 tablespoons sweet butter
2 tablespoons flour
1 cup milk
3 egg yolks
1 teaspoon vanilla extract
4 egg whites

1/8 teaspoon cream of tartar
1/4 cup sugar

GARNISH:
2 tablespoons powdered sugar
2/3 cup heavy cream
1 tablespoon Grand Marnier
1 tablespoon sugar

Butter 8 6-ounce souffle cups. Sprinkle with granulated sugar. Melt chocolate with coffee in double boiler over barely simmering water (or 2 minutes on high in microwave). Stir until smooth. Melt butter in a small saucepan. Add flour and cook briefly. Add milk gradually, whisking continuously until you have a smooth sauce. Continue whisking over medium heat until sauce thickens.

Remove from heat and let cool slightly. Add chocolate and whisk smooth. Mix in egg yolks and vanilla. Beat egg whites with cream of tartar until soft peaks form. Add sugar gradually, beating until whites are stiff but not dry. Fold 1/3 of whites into chocolate mixture to lighten it, then fold in remaining whites. Divide mixture, among the 8 prepared cups, place on a baking sheet and bake on the lower shelf of a 375 degree oven for about 17 minutes.

Whip cream with Grand Marnier and granulated sugar. Remove souffles from oven, dust with powdered sugar and serve immediately with the whipped cream. Serves 8.

Mary Evely, Chef
Simi Winery

Port Chocolate with Chocolate

2 ounces (2 squares) unsweetened
 baking chocolate
1 cup sugar
2 large eggs
1/2 teaspoon vanilla
1/4 teaspoon salt

1/2 cup sifted all purpose flour
1/2 cup chopped walnuts
 (optional)
Port chocolate sauce (see
 below)
1/2 cup unsalted butter

Coarsely chop chocolate squares. Heat butter in a heavy saucepan over medium-low heat until half melted. Add chocolate and stir with a wooden spoon until chocolate and butter are melted and blended. Remove from heat. Stir in sugar, stirring until dissolved. Add eggs, one at a time, and beat with a spoon after each addition until mixture is thoroughly combined and shiny. Stir in vanilla and salt. Stir in flour.

Turn into buttered 9-inch round layer cake pan and spread smooth. Bake in a 350 degree oven until slightly firm to touch and toothpick inserted in center shows mixture is a little moist, about 25 minutes. Let cool in pan on a rack. To serve, cut into wedges and top each with warm sauce. Serves 12. Note: If you want less consistency of pure chocolate, add 1/2 cup chopped walnuts to base batter before baking.

PORT CHOCOLATE SAUCE:

1 package (4 ounces) sweet
 baking chocolate

1/2 cup Port

Combine in top part of double boiler over hot (not boiling) water, the chocolate, coarsely chopped and Port. Heat and whisk until smooth. Makes about 1 cup, or topping for 6 to 8 dessert servings.

Shirley Sarvis, Consultant
Ficklin Vineyards

Shirley Sarvis, who has written more than a dozen cookbooks, created this recipe for Ficklin Vineyards Port Wine. It is a delicious exotic dessert, with intense chocolate flavors in harmony with the spirit and vibrancy of Port wine.

Sonoma Apple Jack Tart

CRUST (MAKES 2 9-INCH TART SHELLS):

2 cups flour
1/4 cup sugar
5 ounces sweet butter, chilled and
  cut into 1/4-inch bits

1 whole egg
1/2 teaspoon salt
1 9-inch tart pan, with
  removable bottom

Combine flour, sugar, salt and butter and quickly mix until it resembles coarse corn meal. Add the egg and quickly mix until it forms a ball. Gather and press dough together, wrap in plastic and chill two hours or overnight. Roll out half the dough and line a 9-inch tart pan. Prick with a fork several times. Freeze the other half of the dough.

FILLING:

4 large Gravenstein or other tart
  apples, peeled, cored and sliced
  (about 4 cups)
1 tablespoon lemon juice
2 tablespoons brown sugar
1 tablespoon sugar

1 tablespoon flour
1 teaspoon cinnamon
1/4 teaspoon freshly grated
  nutmeg
1/8 teaspoon white pepper,
  freshly ground

Mix all ingredients together well and fill the tart shell evenly.

TOPPING:

1/2 cup sugar
1/2 cup flour
3 ounces butter, cut into bits

1/2 cup grated dry jack
  cheese

Combine sugar, flour and butter and rub together with your fingertips until they look like coarse oatmeal. Add cheese and briefly mix.

To finish the tart, preheat oven to 350 degrees. Scatter topping evenly over filled tart. Bake for 40 minutes until top is golden and apples are tender. Cool slightly before serving. Serve with a dollop of vanilla bean ice cream.

Recommended Wine: Fetzer Gewurztraminer. The slightly sweet spicy flavors of the Gewurz bring out the subtle spiciness and appley flavors of this unforgettable desert.

John Ash, Culinary Director
Fetzer Vineyard

Biscotti Sonoma

1 cup sugar
1/2 cup butter, melted
3 tablespoons Champagne
2 tablespoons candied ginger,
 finely minced
1/2 teaspoon ground cinnamon
1 teaspoon vanilla
1 cup toasted walnuts, chopped

3 eggs
2 1/2-3 cups flour
1 1/2 teaspoons baking
 powder
1/4 teaspoon salt
8 ounces semi-sweet melted
 chocolate (optional)

Combine the sugar, butter, Champagne, spices and walnuts. Mix well, then add the dry ingredients.

Form into a 2 1/2 to 3-inch wide loaf. Bake for 25 minutes at 350 degrees.

Cool slightly and slice into 1/2 inch diagonals. Bake 20 more minutes, turning once, until both sides of the cookies are browned.

Cool completely. Dip one side of the cookies in the chocolate, melted in a double boiler, if desired. Store in an air-tight container. Makes 2 1/2 dozen.

Serve with Korbel Champagne/Brut.

**Teresa Douglas/Mitchell, Culinary Director
Korbel Champagne Cellars**

Fruity Port Cake

1 cup sugar	Grated rind of one orange
2 cups flour	1/4 cup orange juice
1 teaspoon cloves	2 teaspoons baking powder
1 1/2 cups dried fruit, chopped, or raisins	1 teaspoon baking soda
1 cup Port wine	1/2 cup margarine, softened, not melted
1 egg beaten	1/2 cup chopped walnuts

(The day or night before baking, soak 1 1/2 cups of chopped dried fruit or raisins in 1 cup Port.)

Mix together sugar, flour, cloves, baking powder and baking soda. Add softened margarine and blend with fork to make fine crumbs. Next, blend in to moisten, but do not overmix: beaten egg, grated orange rind, orange juice, chopped walnuts, chopped fruit and remaining port mixture.

Pour in a 9 inch by 5 inch loaf pan. Bake at 350 degrees for one hour. Serve with Cheddar or Swiss cheese, fresh fruit and Weibel Rare Port.

Diana Weibel
Weibel Vineyards

Coconut Tuiles with Coconut Sorbet, Mango and Hot Fudge Sauces

TUILES:

1/2 cup butter, melted
1 1/2 cups sugar
1 1/2 egg whites

1/4 cup flour, sifted
5-6 cups unsweetened
  coconut

Mix everything in a bowl, let stand 10 minutes at room temperature. Butter a teflon-coated cookie sheet. Place 2-3 tablespoons of batter onto cookie sheet and spread out with fork to a large circle. Bake until golden, approximately 10 minutes.

After cooling slightly, bend around the bottom of a glass to get cupped shape, or use rolling pin for half-round shape.

MANGO SAUCE:

Peel, and cut mango in pieces. Puree in blender with sugar and a little lemon juice to taste.

HOT FUDGE SAUCE:

8 ounces bitter-sweet chocolate
4 ounces unsalted butter

1/4 cup brandy
1/2 cup light corn syrup

Melt chocolate and butter and mix together. Add brandy and corn syrup and cook until desired consistency.

To serve, spoon mango puree on plate. Place tuile on bed of puree with scoop of coconut sorbet in center. Top with hot fudge sauce.

Serve with Scharffenberger N.V. Cremont

Kazuto Matsusaka, Executive Chef
Chinois on Main in Santa Monica, California
for
Scharffenberger Cellars

Apricot Crown

1 cup dried apricots
1/2 cup sugar
1 large egg
1/4 teaspoon grated lemon rind
1 teaspoon lemon juice

1/2 cup chopped toasted
 blanched almonds
2 pounds puff pastry dough
1 egg, lightly beaten

Put apricots in a saucepan with water to cover. Cook over low heat until soft. Drain and puree. Add remaining filling ingredients except nuts. Cool. Divide puff pastry in half. Roll, then cut a circle 10 inches in diameter, 1/4-inch thick and place on parchment lined baking sheet. Roll and cut a circle 11 inches in diameter, 1/4-inch thick.

Sprinkle nuts; mound filling in center 11 inches in diameter, 1/4-inch thick. Sprinkle nuts; mound filling in center of 10-inch circle, leaving a 1 1/2-inch border. Moisten outside edge of base with water. Cover with 11-inch circle. Make a scalloped border by pressing the outside edge of a knife at 2-inch intervals. Cut a small circle in center of pastry. Cut small curving lines from center of circle to outside scallop. Chill 1 hour. Glaze with egg. Bake in preheated 425 degree oven for 30 minutes. Reduce heat to 375 degrees. Bake for 20 minutes or until golden brown. Serves 10 to 12.

Serve while still warm with Freemark Abbey's Edelwein Gold.

Sandra Learned, Consulting Chef
Freemark Abbey Vineyard

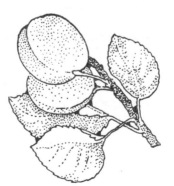

Decadent Chocolate Brownies
with Port Cream

4 ounces unsweetened chocolate
4 ounces semi-sweet chocolate
8 ounces unsalted butter
1 3/4 cups granulated sugar
7 eggs, beaten

1 tablespoon vanilla
1 tablespoon salt
1 cup flour
1/2 cup walnut, chopped
(optional)

Preheat oven to 350 degrees. Generously butter an 8 inch by 13 inch medium baking pan.

Chop chocolate into bits and heat with butter in a double boiler until completely melted. Remove from the heat and stir in sugar to partially dissolve. Beat the eggs with vanilla. Separately sift the flour and salt together. Stir the egg into melted chocolate, and then stir in the flour and walnuts just until combined. Do no over stir. Spread into buttered pan and bake 25 to 30 minutes for soft brownies (40 minutes for chewier brownies).

Cool completely before cutting and serve with a dollop of Port Cream.

PORT CREAM:

1 cup Cabernet Port
1 cup heavy whipping cream

1/4 cup sugar
1 teaspoon vanilla

Simmer the Port over medium-high heat until reduced to 1/4 cup. Then chill.

Beat the cream until just thickening, then stream in the sugar, reduced Port and vanilla. Continue to beat to soft peak.

Enjoy with a glass of Beringer Vineyards Cabernet Port Wine.

Kerry Romaniello, Sous Chef
Beringer Vineyards

Biscotti

6 eggs
2 cups sugar
3 cups sifted flour
3 teaspoons baking powder
Grated lemon rind
1 1/2 cubes melted butter
1 teaspoon vanilla

2 teaspoons almond extract
1 teaspoon (or more) anise
  seed
1 teaspoon anise extract
1 jigger Brandy
1 cup chopped almonds

Cream together eggs, sugar, flour and baking powder. Add the rest of the ingredients. Pour onto greased cookie sheet with edges. Bake at 350 degrees for 30 to 40 minutes. Cut into serving-size biscuits and place each piece on its side on cookie sheet. The biscotti will not all fit on one cookie sheet. Return to oven for a few minutes to brown slowly so they are nice and crunchy. Don't forget to toast both sides.

Perfect for dunking into Sausal Zinfandel or Cabernet.

Roselee Demonstene & Cindy Martin, Co-Owners
Sausal Winery

Zucchini Zinfandel Chocolate Loaf

1 cup unsweetened cocoa
2 eggs
1/2 cup oil
1 cup sugar
2 tablespoons poppy seeds
1/2 cup milk
1 cup zucchini, shredded &
  unpeeled

1/4 cup Zinfandel
2 cups flour
1 teaspoon baking powder
1 teaspoon baking soda
1/2 teaspoon salt
1 teaspoon cinnamon
1/2 teaspoon nutmeg

Stir all ingredients together well and pour into a greased 8X5-inch loaf pan. Bake at 325 degrees for 60 to 70 minutes.

Serve with Martinelli's Zinfandel or Muscat Alexandria.

Julie Martinelli
Martinelli Vineyards

Cinnamon Pumpkin Flan

1 1/4 cups sugar
1/2 teaspoon salt
1 teaspoon cinnamon
1 cup pumpkin
5 large eggs, slightly beaten

2 cups light cream
1/2 pint whipping cream
1/4 teaspoon ginger
2 teaspoons powdered sugar

Melt 1/2 cup of sugar in 9-inch heat-proof glass pie plate over very low heat. Stir constantly until golden syrup forms. Tip plate to cover sides and bottom with syrup and cool. In bowl, combine sugar, salt and cinnamon. Add pumpkin, eggs and light cream. Mix well and pour into caramel-covered pie plate.

Set pie plate in a larger pan and pour in hot water until it comes about 1/2 inch up the outside of the pie plate. Bake at 350 degrees for 1 hour, or until knife comes out clean. Chill.

Unmold plate upside-down onto a dish with a slight rim so the caramel won't spill over the sides. Garnish with a cream made by combining the whipping cream with ginger and powdered sugar. Serves 6.

Serve with Bergfeld Pinot Noir.

Shanna Geiger
for
Bergfeld Winery

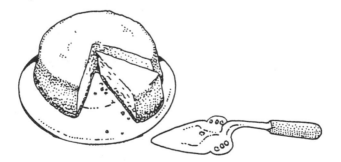

Creama Catalana

3 cups milk
Peel of 1 lemon, pith removed
2 cinnamon sticks (3 inches each)

6 egg yolks
10 tablespoons sugar
3 tablespoons cornstarch

Bring milk to boil with lemon peel and cinnamon sticks; reduce heat to low. Simmer, stirring occasionally, 10 minutes. Remove cinnamon sticks and lemon peel and discard. In top of double boiler, beat egg yolks and 4 tablespoons of the sugar together until light and lemon colored; beat in cornstarch until smooth. Add 1/2 cup of the milk, stirring constantly with wooden spoon until smooth, and until custard coats a spoon, about 20 minutes. Divide custard evenly into 6 oven-proof dessert cups. Chill custard thoroughly, about 3 hours. Just before serving, sprinkle 1 tablespoon of remaining sugar over each serving. Set cups 4 to 5 inches away from a moderately hot broiler; broil until sugar is brown and caramelized, about 5 minutes. Serves 6.

Recommended wine: Gloria Ferrer 1986 Royal Cuvée.

Gloria Ferrer Champagne Caves

Raspberry Sorbet

1 cup water
2 pints raspberries
1 teaspoon lemon juice

2/3 cup sugar
1 egg white, lightly beaten

In large saucepan, heat water and sugar to boiling, add raspberries. Transfer to food processor and puree. Strain into a large bowl and refrigerate until cold, 20 minutes. Just before freezing, whisk beaten egg white and lemon juice into the chilled puree. Freeze in an ice-cream maker according to manufacturer's directions. Makes 6 cups, 65 calories per 1/2 cup. Great color, great taste, perfect for a hot summer day.

**Carol Kozlowski-Every
Kozlowski Farms**

Chilled Chocolate Tortoni

8 ounces (1 package) semi-sweet chocolate
2/3 cup Karo light or dark corn syrup
2 cups heavy cream, divided

1 1/2 cups broken chocolate wafers or other crisp cookies
1 cup coarsely chopped walnuts

Line 12 muffin cups with paper liners. In 3 quart saucepan, stir chocolate and corn syrup over low heat, just until chocolate melts; remove from heat. Stir in 1/2 cup of heavy cream until blended. Refrigerate 15 minutes or until cool.

Beat remaining cream until soft peaks form; gently stir into chocolate mixture. Stir in cookies and nuts. Spoon into muffin cups.

Freeze 4 to 6 hours or until firm. Garnish as desired. Let stand a few minutes before serving. Store covered in freezer up to 1 month. Serves 12.

Recommended wine: Foppiano Reserve Zinfandel -- 1987.

Susan Foppiano
Foppiano Vineyards

Brandied Pear and Cranberry Pie

4 cups firm pears, peeled and cubed (Bartlett or Bosc)	3/4 cup sugar
1 cup cranberries	1 lemon, zested and juiced
3/4 cup chopped toasted walnuts	1/2 cup Brandy
1 pinch of cinnamon	1/4 cup flour
	2 tablespoons butter

Mix all ingredients, except butter, and let marinade 15 minutes.

Pour into a 9-inch unbaked pie shell, dot with butter, and cover with an upper crust with steam vents cut out. Crimp edges and sprinkle with cinnamon sugar.

Bake on a baking stone for 10 minutes at 450 degrees, then lower temperature to 350 and bake another 20 to 30 minutes.

Serve with cream while still warm. Serves 6 to 8.

Michele Mutrux
for
Carneros Alambic Distillery

Quick and Easy Wine Cake

1 package yellow cake mix	3/4 cup oil
1 4 1/2-ounce package instant vanilla pudding	3/4 Grey Reisling or cocktail sherry
4 eggs	1 teaspoon nutmeg

Combine all ingredients, mix with electric beater about 5 minutes, at medium speed. Pour batter into greased bundt cake pan and bake in 350 degree oven for 45 minutes or until done.

Jeani Martini pairs this quick and easy dessert with their Fountain Grove Grey Reisling for instant entertaining.

Jeani Martini
Martini & Prati Wines

Spicy Peppernuts

1 cup brown sugar, packed
4 tablespoons butter, softened
1 egg
1 teaspoon brandy
1 3/4 cups flour

1/4 teaspoon baking soda
1/4 teaspoon cloves
1/4 teaspoon ginger
1/4 teaspoon cinnamon
1/4 teaspoon pepper

Cream butter and brown sugar. Stir in egg and brandy. Mix dry ingredients and add, mixing with hands. Shape into balls and place 1 inch apart on baking sheet. Bake in 375 degree oven for 8 minutes or until lightly browned. Keep covered tightly in tin or store in deep freeze. Makes 70.

Serve with Quivira Zinfandel.

Holly P. Wendt, Proprietor
Quivira Vineyards

Rhubarb-Berry Soup

6-8 stalks rhubarb
Grape juice (optional)
Sugar to taste
2 tablespoons cornstarch

1 teaspoon vanilla
1 pint raspberries or
  strawberries
Whipped cream (garnish)

Cut 6 to 8 stalks of rhubarb into 1-inch pieces. Cover with grape juice (or water) and simmer for about 20 minutes. Cool slightly and process in blender or food processor. Return to pot and add sugar to taste (very little if you use grape juice, more if you use water). Bring to a simmer and thicken with 2 tablespoons cornstarch, dissolved in 1/4 cup of water. Add 1 pint raspberries or strawberries and 1 teaspoon vanilla. Serve chilled with a dollop of whipped cream. Serves 6.

Serve with Cluster Select Late Harvest Gewurztraminer.

Navarro Vineyards

Pinot Noir Pomegranate Sorbet

1 cup Pinot Noir
1 cup pomegranate juice (strained)
2 cups water

3 tablespoons granulated
sugar
1/2 cup grapefruit juice
(strained)

Combine 1/2 cup of water and sugar in a saucepan. Bring to a boil and cool to room temperature. Mix together the Pinot Noir, pomegranate juice, grapefruit juice and remaining water. Add the sugar syrup and mix well. Freeze in a shallow pan until solid. Empty the frozen mixture into the food processor. Process on pulse just until the texture is consistent, then freeze again in a covered plastic container. If you have an ice cream maker, follow the manufacturer's directions for sorbet, then transfer to a plastic container. If kept airtight and frozen, the sorbet will last for 3 to 4 days. Serves 6.

This simple dessert is perfect after a fish course or refreshing as a dessert in itself. Follow it with a glass of Greenwood Ridge Vineyards Anderson Valley Pinot Noir.

Dony Kwan
for
Greenwood Ridge Vineyards

Poached Muscat Pears

2 pears, cut in half, cored, leaving a good sized hole - leave skin on
1/2 cup chopped walnuts
Butter lettuce for garnish

Saute pears on both sides in small amount of butter. Add chopped walnuts and 1/2 cup Muscat wine. Cover and poach 5 minutes or until pears are still firm. Refrigerate overnight. Place pears on bed of butter lettuce, sprinkle with more walnuts and Muscat. Top with whipped cream and a cherry. Serves 4.

Jeani Martini
Martini & Prati Wines

Cold Lemon Souffle

1 envelope gelatin	1/4 cup sugar
2 tablespoons cold water	4 egg whites
1/2 cup lemon juice	1/4 cup sugar
1 tablespoon lemon zest	1 cup heavy whipping cream
4 egg yolks	

Soften gelatin in cold water. Add lemon juice and heat only until gelatin dissolves. Remove from heat and add zest.

Whip egg yolks and 1/4 cup sugar until they become thick and pale. Whip in gelatin mixture.

Whip egg whites until foamy. Gradually add sugar and continue whipping until thick and glossy.

Add some of the yolks to the whites and mix. Then add all of the whites to the yolks.

Whip 1 cup heavy whipping cream until stiff and fold into lemon and egg mixture. This is good served with raspberry sauce. Serves 4 to 6.

Serve with Kenwood Vineyards Chenin Blanc.

A recipe from the Kenwood Collection
Kenwood Vineyards

Poached Pears a la Zinfandel

6-8 pears
2 cups Zinfandel
1/2 cup sugar
Lemon peel

1 cup sour cream (or plain
 yogurt)
2 tablespoons sugar
1/2 teaspoon vanilla
Dash of salt

PEARS:

Combine and heat in covered pot until sugar dissolves, 2 cups Zinfandel and 1/2 cup sugar. Place 6 to 8 medium peeled pears with stems attached and 4 thin strips of lemon peel with wine/sugar in crock pot. Cook low for 6 to 8 hours, turning occasionally until pears are very soft.

TOPPING:

Place 1 cup sour cream (or plain yogurt) in a bowl in the freezer (also place beaters in freezer). When crystals begin to form around the edge of the cream or yogurt (about 2 hours) add 2 tablespoons of sugar, a dash of salt, 1/2 teaspoon of vanilla, and beat with chilled beaters on high for 4 to 5 minutes. Serve over warm pears along with the Hop Kiln 1991 Late Harvest Zinfandel.

**Hop Kiln Winery
at
Griffin Vineyard**

INDEX
OF
RECIPES

INDEX

Postscript . . .

Additional copies of this book are available for $15.95, which includes shipping and handling.

The illustration on the cover of this book is available as a poster, 22 by 28 inches, in full color, and signed by Ellie Marshall, distinguished California Wine Country artist. It is ready for framing. The cost is $29.95, including shipping and handling.

A miniature of the same scene, 5 X 7 inches, in full color, also suitable for framing, is available for $11.95, including shipping and handling.

Send your personal check or money order to: The Hoffman Press, P.O. Box 2996, Santa Rosa, CA 95405. Your money back if you are not delighted.